BOSTON TERRIER
AND
BOSTON TERRIERS

Boston Terrier
Total Guide

BOSTON TERRIER, BOSTON TERRIER PUPPIES, BOSTON TERRIERS, BOSTON TERRIER DOGS, BOSTON TERRIER TRAINING, BREEDERS, HEALTH & MORE!

Susanne Saben

© DYM Worldwide Publishers

DYM Worldwide Publishers

ISBN: 978-1-911355-67-0

will not be liable for, the websites being temporary or being removed from the Internet. The accuracy and completeness of the information provided herein, and opinions stated herein are not guaranteed or warranted to produce any particular results, and the advice or strategies contained herein may not be suitable for every individual. The author, publisher, distributors, and/or affiliates shall not be liable for any loss incurred as a consequence of the use and application, directly or indirectly of any information presented in this work. This publication is designed to provide information regarding the subject matter covered. The information included in this book has been compiled to give an overview of the topics covered. The information contained in this book has been compiled to provide an overview of the subject. It is not intended as medical advice and should not be construed as such. For a firm diagnosis of any medical conditions, you should consult a doctor or veterinarian (as related to animal health). The writer, publisher, distributors, and/or affiliates of this work are not responsible for any damages or negative consequences following any of the treatments or methods highlighted in this book. Website links are for informational purposes only and should not be seen as a personal endorsement; the same applies to any products or services mentioned in this work. The reader should also be aware that although the web links included were correct at the time of writing they may become out of date in the future. Any pricing or currency exchange rate information was accurate at the time of writing but may become out of date in the future. The Author, Publisher, distributors, and/or affiliates assume no responsibility for pricing and currency exchange rates mentioned within this work.

Table of Contents

Introduction
to the Boston Terrier

I can't remember a time in my life when I did not own a dog! I've owned Beagles, Maltese, and American Bulldogs. However, it was not until I was a young adult that I was introduced to the dog that would become my favorite breed – the Boston Terrier.

Boston Terriers (also known as "Bostons" or "Bosties") have a personality all their own. Many dogs are loyal, energetic, and affectionate. Those adjectives describe the Boston, but there is so much more that makes the breed special. Perhaps it is the way that Bosties bond with their families. Maybe it is the positive energy that a Boston exhibits. It could be the ability of the Boston to go from hyperactive play to sitting patiently on his owner's lap. Regardless, the Boston Terrier is an extraordinary dog.

Throughout this book, we will explore the variations of the Boston Terrier – breed standards and colors, Boston Terrier mixes, and the different sizes of Boston Terriers. We will also discuss health issues, training, and finding the right Boston for your family.

I have personally owned five Boston Terriers over the years. I have had newborn Bostons, and I have taken in Bostons who might otherwise have been left to sit indefinitely in a pen outdoors. I have worked personally with each of our dogs. However, much of my knowledge about Bostons is based on research as well! Many things I will share with you via this book are research-based ideas that I have personally tried with my pups.

I sincerely hope that this book provides not only enjoyment in reading but is also helpful. If you are considering purchasing a Boston or adopting, (many awesome dogs are available at Boston Terrier rescues), you are about to embark on a wonderful journey. If you have already brought home your little bundle of Boston Terrier joy, then I hope that this book will assist you with any issue you may encounter as a new pet parent.

I sincerely thank you for purchasing this book! Best of luck as you bring your new Bostie home, and here's wishing you many, many years of companionship with one of the best dog breeds available.

CHAPTER 1

What Were Boston Terriers Originally Bred For?

Figure 1: Adult Boston Terrier

The Boston Terrier is a fairly new dog breed. Two separate stories exist regarding the origin of the Boston Terrier. While most experts agree that all modern Boston Terriers are descended from a dog named Judge, some historians differ on how Judge's owner, Robert C. Hooper, procured the dog.

We do know that Hooper obtained Judge around 1870. However, stories differ after this date. Some historians state that Hooper, a Bostonian, imported a cross between a Bulldog and the now-extinct English Terrier from England. This dog is purported to be Judge, whom Hooper would later breed to Burnett's Gyp – we will return to that story momentarily. Other stories report that Hooper purchased Judge from a fellow Bostonian, William O'Brian. The only certainty that we have from records kept by Hooper is that he did indeed own a dog named Judge and that Judge was bred to Burnett's Gyp. Burnett's Gyp is often referred to as "Kate" in historical documents. The explanation for this is that her formal name – what is found on registration papers – is Burnett's Gyp. However, her family referred to her as Kate.

Figure 2: Map of Boston – The hometown of the Boston Terrier

Out of this union came one pup – a male. He was given the name Well's Eph.

Judge and Kate would have been larger in size than the typical Boston Terrier of today. According to *The Complete Dog Book*, Judge was "a well-built, high-stationed dog." He weighed a little over thirty pounds. He was brindle in color, and his square, block-shaped head was set off by a white blaze down his face. Kate was a white dog (some historians claim that Kate was an

English Terrier; there is no concrete evidence of this, however).
Kate weighed roughly twenty pounds. No other evidence exists
regarding her looks or size.

Fig. 38.—BULL TERRIER, TARQUIN.

Figure 3: A Terrier that might resemble Kate.

Surprisingly, many historical accounts paint Well's Eph as "not
very attractive." No exact details are given about this, so it is
difficult to guess what Well's Eph looked exactly like. However,
his lack of good looks did not stop his owner from breeding
him. In fact, we are told that Well's Eph might not have been
handsome, but he had some great character traits that enticed
several breeders.

In the lineage of Boston Terriers, Well's Eph was bred to a female
known to us as "Tobin's Kate." This Kate weighed twenty pounds

and had a "fairly short head." She was a golden brindle color. Historians believe that Eph and Kate produced offspring that was interbred with French Bulldogs, and this is the foundation of the Boston Terrier we know today.

Although Robert C. Hooper and Edward Burnett are credited with creating the foundation of the Boston Terrier breed, they did not christen the breed with that name. Considering that Eph's offspring likely exhibited a short, square head, many of his descendants were referred to as round heads, bullet heads, or round-headed bull-and-terriers. Some owners referred to their pups as Boston Bull Terriers. In 1889, approximately thirty Boston Bull Terrier fanciers came together to form the American Bull Terrier Club. At this point, the club deemed the dog Round Heads or Bull Terriers. However, a breed referred to as the Bull Terrier already existed, so the club found themselves reinventing the dog's moniker once again. They dropped the "Bull" from the dog's name and became the Boston Terrier Club. Four years later, in 1893, the American Kennel Club (AKC) recognized the Boston Terrier. It was the first "made-in-America" breed registered by the AKC.

The Boston was never meant to be a true working dog; however, he is most definitely a "terrier." Terriers of all varieties are particularly drawn to hunt small animals. At one point in the early years of the breed, the Boston Terrier was used as a "ratter," which means he was trained to hunt and kill rats. In fact, more than one Boston pet parent has related stories of their pup chasing squirrels. However, today's Boston Terrier pet is strictly a companion, not a hunter.

Figure 4: The Boston Terrier with an American flag

Why is the Boston Terrier "A Truly American Dog"?

The Boston Terrier is truly an American dog because the breed was developed in the United States. The "Boston" in his name is a nod to his birthplace. Robert Hooper was a native of Boston, Massachusetts. Kate's owner, Edward Burnett, hailed from Southboro, Massachusetts (roughly thirty miles separate the two locations). Well's Eph, the offspring of Judge and Kate, was bred many times, but generally within a short distance of Boston.

Because of his origins, the Boston Terrier is truly American made. His nickname, "The American Gentleman," refers to the tuxedo-style coat pattern of the Boston. While there are variations of the Boston Terrier in color today, in his beginnings, he was generally black and white or brindle and white. (Brindle is a color pattern that is often brown with streaks of other colors, such as red and fawn, mixed into the pattern.) His dark coat contrasted with white markings on his face, chest, and stomach. This pattern of markings resembled that of a tuxedo; hence the nickname.

Some historians claim that Judge himself was half Bulldog and half English Terrier. Others state that Judge was a Bull Terrier himself and that Kate was the English Terrier. Still, others believe Judge had English Bulldog genetics in his bloodline. While no one is certain if Judge was imported from England or if he was actually born in the United States, his progeny does hail from America.

Is there such a thing as an Old Boston Terrier?

Today, the Boston Terrier is a relatively small dog weighing less than twenty-five pounds. However, as the breed was being developed, particularly during the time of the "round head" dogs, the Boston was somewhat larger. The Old Boston Terrier, also known as the Olde Boston Bulldogge, is related to Judge and his descendants. He would have been the version of the Boston Terrier prior to interbreeding with the French Bulldog. Because there are so many discrepancies regarding the exact history of the Boston Terrier, we should also consider this incarnation of the Boston Terrier.

Surprisingly enough, the Olde Boston Bulldogge was possibly bred for dogfighting. We know for certain that this version of the Boston Terrier was a cross between an English Bulldog, the Bull Terrier, and the White English Terrier (again, the English Terrier is now extinct). Experts tell us that some of the resulting pups of this interbreeding had a typical long head of a terrier, while some inherited the round head of the Bulldog parent breed.

Most experts agree that this is the version of the dog that was crossbred with French Bulldogs to bring about a smaller dog with all the tenacity of the Boston Bulldogge.

What is the difference between a Boston Terrier and a Boston Bulldog?

With the introduction of the French Bulldog, the Boston Terrier was created. However, the Old Boston Bulldogge (or Boston Bulldog) is still in existence. It is not a very widely known breed, and it is not recognized by the American Kennel Club. The Boston Bulldog is indeed a separate breed; however, many Boston Terriers do look very much like the Old Boston Bulldogge. This version of the Boston Bulldog is what was named the "round-headed Bull and Terrier of Boston." The Boston Bulldog is larger than the Boston Terrier. He will weigh anywhere from twenty-five to forty-five pounds (11.3 to 20.3 kg). He is also taller at the shoulder than a Boston Terrier; however, his exact height varies.

The Old Boston Bulldogge has much the same temperament as the Boston Terrier. He is affectionate with his family, and he is also highly protective. Like the Boston Terrier, he is easily trained. Some owners even brag that the Old Boston Bulldogge enjoys learning and performing tricks. Often, the Boston Bulldog, Old Boston Bulldogge, and the Old Boston dogs are all different names referring to the same dog.

CHAPTER 2

Is the Boston Terrier Right for You?

Certainly, the Boston Terrier is an adorable little dog. Most owners agree that he is an excellent dog, with a great personality and energy level to match. However, you still might be questioning whether or not the Boston Terrier is the right dog for *you*. Let's look at some of the characteristics that make the Boston Terrier such a fantastic dog.

Is the Boston Terrier a Good Companion?

First, the Boston Terrier is a great dog whether you are single or attached. They partners well with or without children. Everyone finds the Boston Terrier to be a great companion. If you are single, the Boston is great company! He will greet you daily as you return from work with the enthusiasm of a small child. He will join you for walks around the neighborhood, and he is just as satisfied to sit on your lap.

Parents with small children will never need to worry that the Boston Terrier might harm their young ones. While many breeds are good with children, the Boston seems to have a special predisposition to love kids. When my children were very young, our Boston at the time exhibited much patience. My child could pull her ears or hug too tightly, but the dog seemed to sense that the child did not mean to harm her. The dog was also very protective of my child. She would put herself between guests in our home and the child. She never bit anyone, but we noticed that the dog was very watchful. As time passed, the two became great friends.

Moreover, Bostons seem to know that a child in the family is a playmate. Children will often play fetch until the dog tires of the game (which they rarely do!). The Boston Terrier is also highly affectionate with *all* members of the family. In fact, they will often find ways to be close to you. This includes following you throughout the house, sitting beside your feet as you prepare food in the kitchen (there is always the hope that you will drop a morsel), and hanging out in the bathroom while you shower. Boston Terriers are truly devoted to their pet parents!

Figure 5: Boston Terrier playing Tug-of-War

Is the Boston Terrier Intelligent?

The Boston Terrier is absolutely one of the most intelligent breeds. This will help in housebreaking and crate training. In addition, the Boston Terrier is highly intuitive. He will pick up on your emotions. The Boston genuinely wants to please his owner, which is why using praise and rewards to facilitate training is such a great idea.

Figure 6: The Boston Terrier is a highly intelligent dog

Will the Boston Terrier require a lot of Maintenance?

The Boston Terrier requires very little in the way of maintenance. He sheds minimally throughout the year; however, you may notice that he tends to shed more during the spring and fall months. The Boston Terrier does not require regular bathing; in fact, it might be a good idea to bathe him only when he has had a good roll in the dirt or mud (and he may be guilty of doing so on a regular basis!)

He should only be brushed once or twice a month (more during shedding season). Overall, the Boston Terrier makes an excellent dog for those who do not want to commit to a high-maintenance dog.

What is the Weight of a Full-grown Boston Terrier?

Generally, a healthy Boston Terrier weighs about twenty to twenty-five pounds.

Does the Boston Terrier Suffer from Separation Anxiety?

To be frank, the Boston Terrier does have a bit more of a tendency to experience anxiety when you are away, even if you are only gone a few hours to run errands. This is why I recommend crate training. Should you need to be away, place a toy and perhaps a favorite blanket inside the crate. The coziness of the crate will help the Boston to feel more secure while you are at work or running errands. Also, consider the crate as a safety measure. As long as your puppy is in the crate, he can't get into mischief (such as eating something harmful).

Figure 7: A Boston Terrier with separation anxiety

Will I Need to be Active in Order to Own a Boston Terrier?

Not necessarily. The Boston Terrier tends to be more active in spurts if you will. He may run and play for thirty minutes, but then he is ready to rest a bit.

Figure 8: Boston Terrier at play

Truthfully, it is better for the Boston Terrier if you break down his exercise activity into several opportunities throughout the day. This is to accommodate his brachycephalic nose and narrow airways. Often, a short brisk walk around the neighborhood once or twice a day will provide sufficient activity for the Boston Terrier. If you can add some tug-of-war or fetch while you are indoors, you will provide your pup with activity as well as deepen your bond. Try to maintain at least one daily half-hour play session or walk with your Boston Terrier, especially as he ages. Bostons tend to put on weight as they mature, particularly if they do not receive the proper amount of exercise.

Can the Boston Terrier be Stubborn?

Unfortunately, the Boston Terrier can be somewhat stubborn.
Like other terriers, he can be an independent thinker at times.
Keep being persistent and reward him when he does behave. The
key is to motivate your Boston to *want* to obey your commands.
Treats and praise can help you in achieving this goal. Remember,
your Boston will want to please you, and this desire often
motivates him much more than his idea of independence.

Is the Boston Terrier Difficult to Housebreak?

Overall, no. Keep in mind that every dog, regardless of breed,
is different. I have learned from experience that housebreaking
requires patience and consistency. Wait until your puppy is about
ten – to – twelve weeks old before you begin to really emphasize
potty training. I find that the extra maturity in the puppy will
help in his willingness to do what you ask of him. Until he
has reached this age, work with him using a puppy pad. (More
pointers for housebreaking are located in chapter 8.)

Will my Boston Terrier Need to be Socialized?

Socializing your Boston means exposing your young dog to
a variety of situations so that he will know how to behave.
Primarily, you should concentrate on giving your pup the
opportunity to spend time with children and other dogs.
However, this is only the beginning of socializing your dog.

Be sure that you handle your dog and give him the opportunity
to interact with all kinds of people – young and old. When
interacting with your dog, touch his ears and feet. This will help
prepare him for grooming rituals, later on.

Expose him to a variety of sights and sounds. If you do not have children, play sound clips of children laughing and playing (even add a few squeals in there). If you like to watch sports on television, allow him to hear the sportscasters call an exciting game. Listen to the radio at normal volume. Acclimate him to sounds that he is likely to hear as he grows so that he is not frightened later on. You might even play a sound clip from a thunderstorm so that he does not develop a fear of thunder.

It is highly important to expose your pup to children of all ages if there are none already present in your home. Remember, the Boston already has a natural propensity to love children, but never leave your pup unattended with a child. Experts especially recommend exposing your pup to men and responsible children. NOTE: I have noticed that some older dogs will become shy around people with glasses if they aren't accustomed to seeing family members wearing them. You might, on occasion, wear sunglasses or reading glasses, just to expose your puppy to the difference.

Some experts also recommend doing "food bowl exercises" with your young dog. As your dog is eating, approach his bowl. Pet him and drop a treat in the dish. Repeat this over the course of two or three days until you notice that your pup is visibly excited about your approaching him as he eats. This will prevent your dog from exhibiting guarding behavior, which is essential if you have small children who might not be old enough to understand that they should not bother a dog while he's eating.

Although the Boston Terrier is born with a highly congenial personality, a minimum amount of socialization will only add to the friendliness of the dog. Early socialization will also help you avoid behavioral problems as your dog ages.

What is the Cost of Owning a Boston Terrier?

Owning a pet can be expensive. However, the Boston Terrier is a relatively healthy, low-maintenance dog. Here is a general list of typical expenses for the first year of dog ownership:

- Spaying/neutering: $200
- Medical exams with vaccinations: $350
- Harness and collar: $30
- Crate: $50
- Traveling carrier: $50
- Obedience school: $100 (or more)

Let's also take a look at annual (yearly) costs of dog ownership:

- Food: $150
- Regular Vet Exams: $200
- Toys and Treats: $50
- License: $10
- Pet Health Insurance: $225
- Miscellaneous: $50

This adds up to $1500.00 for the first year, not including the price of the dog. Thereafter, you can estimate about $700 per year. NOTE: Should you opt to purchase pet insurance, you may be able to lower the cost of your veterinarian bills.

Keep in mind that these numbers are merely estimates. You can always lower food and prices by buying in bulk; prices on durable toys will vary.)

Prices for food, toys, and insurance may vary based on your location.

Should I Choose a Male or a Female Boston Terrier?

Gender is not an indicator of personality traits where the Boston Terrier is concerned. Males can be cuddly, and females can be somewhat independent. Both genders are friendly, loving, and playful. Much of your dog's behavior is dependent upon how you interact with him as he grows, which is really what socialization is all about. Terriers as a group are often independent thinkers, regardless of gender.

Let me also reassure you at this point that I have owned several types of dogs throughout my life, but the Boston Terrier is, by far, my favorite. Boston Terriers are truly fun to play with, but, at the same time, they make wonderful lap dogs. They are much sturdier than other small dogs such as the Yorkshire Terrier or the Miniature Pinscher (both the Yorkie and the Mini Pin are not recommended for families with small children. This does not apply to the Boston Terrier.)

The Boston Terrier is sweet, intelligent, and playful. He can be highly entertaining, and frequent guests in your home will likely befriend your pup. He is the perfect dog for someone who wants a small dog that does not require a lot of grooming. He will bond with all members of your family, and he becomes fast friends with children. You can never go wrong when choosing a Boston Terrier best friend.

CHAPTER 3

Where Can I Find Boston Terrier Puppies for Sale?

A quick internet search will yield a number of Boston Terrier breeders across the United States, and I have provided a Trusted List in the Bonus Chapter at the end of the book. However, how does one determine whether or not those listed on a typical internet search are reputable breeders?

The Boston Terrier Club of America defines a reputable breeder as one "who is breeding to improve and preserve the breed." Of course, it can be difficult to determine this simply by viewing a breeder's website. However, there IS one good way of determining whether a breeder is trustworthy. Study the breeder's website or page carefully. Look for a health guarantee or the mention of a sales contract. Those two factors are a good sign that the breeder truly has the best interest of the breed at heart.

Another sign that the breeder you are in contact with is reputable is the requirement of an application for possible adoptive parents. This application will ask questions about your family, your experience with dogs, your living arrangements. You may even be questioned about your work schedule. The reputable breeder may be in a business situation, but he or she still cares about the puppies and wants to ensure that they go to good homes.

Keep in mind that even though a breeder may provide a health guarantee, he or she cannot predict every health issue that a dog might have, particularly if there have been no issues in the direct parents of the pups. A trustworthy breeder will have health records on the parents, and he will be honest with you about any possible health issues your potential puppy might experience.

Breeders will often invest in genetic testing for their breeding stock. The Orthopedic Foundation for Animals (OFA) offers health certifications for conditions involving the joints such as patellar luxation and elbow dysplasia. TIP: You can verify certifications through the OFA online at http://www.offa.org. Other genetic testing is done through the Canine Eye Registry Foundation, which certifies that the eyes are normal. Feel free to inquire about these health certifications as you interview breeders. NOTE: These certifications prove that the breeding stock is free from (or are genetic carriers) of these diseases, not the puppy itself. However, one can reasonably assume that since the parents are disease-free, the pups will be, as well.

The Boston Terrier Club of America seems to frown on breeders who advertise through the newspaper or via social media; however, in my area, in particular, there are not an abundance of Boston Terrier breeders. Since this is the case, what can you do to ensure that you find a trustworthy breeder?

- Create a list of questions for the breeder; have the list handy when you contact the breeder, and feel free to ask lots of questions.

- Ask about a health guarantee. For some breeders, this may be a period of six months. Others may guarantee the puppy's health up to a year. On rare occasions, some breeders will guarantee the health of the puppy for a lifetime.

- If possible, schedule a visit to the breeding facility. If you are taken onto the breeder's property and find yourself looking at several animals in unsanitary and unhealthy surroundings (often stacked cages), then thank the breeder for his time and walk away. Unfortunately, starting life in a facility such as this can impact the health of your pup in later years.

- Keep in mind that Boston Terriers, in particular, need to live indoors. They cannot handle extreme weather conditions, and they should not be kept outside. Does that mean that you should not buy from a breeder who does not have a grand indoor facility? Not necessarily.

- Facilities should be clean, first and foremost. You can ask for pictures of the parents (if they are not available on site).

- The breeder may present you with a sales contract. Included in this agreement is the health guarantee (don't be surprised if this covers only a certain time period; no breeder can guarantee a dog will live a certain number of years), and a promise that you will return the dog to the breeder should problems arise.

- Also, the contract will include any health treatments (first set of shots, etc.) that the puppy will receive prior to leaving the breeder for its new home.

You can also ask the breeder for references from previous customers.

You may be thinking, "What if I am unable to travel to the breeder's facilities?" Always, *always* use caution when searching online for a puppy. Although you can't see the facilities, you can still ask for a sales contract, references, and pictures of the puppy's parents. Be careful about sending deposits without any type of written guarantee from the breeder. In today's world of social media, pictures can be stolen from a breeder's website or social media page, and potential customers can be duped into sending deposits. Become a member of social media groups dedicated to a breed. You will find enthusiasts that can be trusted within the group. Also, you can ask these trusted enthusiasts for a "virtual" word-of-mouth breeder recommendation.

Never send cash to make a deposit on a puppy – only use methods of sending money that can be recouped, should you fall victim of a scammer.

Finally, from personal experience, trust your instincts. If a breeder seems too good to be true – a low price, unlimited registration, no contract, no questions asked – then you are likely walking into a negative situation. Ask lots of questions and do your homework on the breeder.

What is the Typical Boston Terrier Price?

Boston Terrier price will be determined by whether or not the dog is registered (and with what organization). Dogs with a limited registration (you will sign a contract that you will not breed the dog) are somewhat cheaper than a dog with unlimited registration (you will be, in essence, purchasing the ability to breed your dog at a later date and register them).

Most Boston Terriers can range in price from $500 - $1,500.00. A show-quality dog may carry a price tag of $2,000.00 or more. If the breeder will need to ship your dog, expect up to an extra $400 added to that cost.

The price of the Boston Terrier varies from state – to –state and region – to – region across the United States. Some breeders, particularly those in more rural areas, sell their Boston Terrier for $300 to $500. This price includes registration papers. By the same token, breeders in the same area may sell a registered Boston Terrier for $1200.00 - $1500.00. Often, this depends on the level of experience the breeder has and whether or not the breeder is more of a hobbyist or a full-time breeder. Those who breed simply out of love for the breed often sell their dogs at a cheaper rate. This does not mean that a Boston Terrier you purchase from a hobbyist is of any lesser quality than a Boston you obtain from a full-time breeder. You will need to check out the breeder's facilities and meet the parents to ascertain whether the dog is a quality, well-bred pup.

Where Can I Find Boston Terrier Puppies for Sale Near Me?

Although The Boston Terrier Club of America advises against doing so, checking the classifieds in the newspaper, searching through trustworthy sites, (please see the bonus chapter for a list of reputable websites), or simply running an internet search will net you plenty of names of breeders near your location. However,

I also recommend word – of – mouth advertising as well. This is somewhat safer than an anonymous web search. The American Kennel Club's website has a list of reputable breeders, as does the Boston Terrier Club of America's site.

What about any Boston Terriers for Sale Near Me?

Again, word-of-mouth advertising works well in this situation. Remember, if you do search via the web, ask the breeder lots of questions. Often, older Bostons for sale are just what a reputable breeder tries to prevent – the rehoming of an older puppy simply because a person decided the Boston had too much energy, or perhaps they were a little too destructive. You can still obtain a healthy dog in this way, but you will not have the health guarantee you would have if you were able to purchase the puppy at a young age. Should you decide to purchase an older Boston Terrier, ask for all paperwork from the veterinarian, regarding exams. You can get an idea of the dog's health history by obtaining this paperwork.

The great thing about Bostons is that they bond with their owners at any age. I recently obtained a five-year-old that I suspect was part of a puppy mill. The first week was hard – she had had her puppies taken from her (which can result in a bit of a depression for a Boston mom), and she was in a totally new place with new people. She was scared. She would not eat, drink water, or go to the bathroom. However, within a week, she began to let her guard down a bit. If you choose to purchase an older Boston, you may have a similar experience until the dog becomes acclimated to you. However, you won't find a more loyal friend once the adult Boston bonds to you. Be consistent. Establish routine feeding and play times. Soon, he will feel right at home!

Is it Possible to Find Miniature Boston Terriers for Sale?

Yes, a quick Internet search provides you with a list of breeders of Miniature Boston Terriers. However, use the same criteria to determine if these are reputable breeders. Use caution when sending a deposit, and make sure you will be given a sales contract. Often, because these dogs are a novelty, you may pay a higher price for a Miniature Boston. Also, be sure to talk with the breeders about health issues.

How Can I Find Teacup Boston Terriers for Sale?

Teacup Boston Terriers are fairly rare, as are miniature Boston Terriers. You should do an Internet search to find a list of breeders, then make a point to either view their facilities or at the very least, do a phone interview with the breeder. Ask about health guarantees, pictures of the parents, and breeder references. Remember to steer clear of any breeder that cannot provide you with these things.

Where Can I Buy Toy-Sized Boston Terriers?

There are breeders who cater to the miniature and toy-sized versions of the Boston Terrier. Again, do your research. Ask for recommendations from people you trust. Conduct an interview with the breeder asking for health guarantees, a sales contract, and pictures of the parents.

Some breeders do not recognize the toy or miniature versions of a Boston Terrier. Keep in mind that the Boston Terrier is already a rather small dog. According to these breeders, since the American Kennel Club does not recognize toy-sized or miniature Boston Terriers, breeders should not market this variation of the Boston Terrier.

Of course, Boston Terrier puppies are very small to begin with. Experts warn of breeders who simply pass off a regular puppy as a toy-sized or teacup variation of the breed. Those who offer teacup, toy, or miniature versions of the Boston Terrier may play up their rarity, and they may charge up to $3,000.00 for the novelty of the small dog.

In the interest of full disclosure, some disreputable breeders will simply mate two very small dogs – often referred to as the "runt" of the litter – to achieve a Boston Terrier weighing less than ten pounds.

While being the "runt" of the litter does not mean that the pup is destined to experience health problems, it is documented that they often have weaker bones than their more "normal-sized" siblings. Also, they often lack natural antibodies. This is no fault of the puppy; often, bigger puppies will push their smaller siblings away from the mother during feeding time. Some "runts" are bottle-fed because of this, and they are not exposed to the mother's natural immunity. These tiny pups may experience issues with hypoglycemia (low blood sugar), hydrocephalus (water on the brain), in addition to heart and respiratory problems. In addition, teacup dogs may need to be fed several times a day, due to digestive issues. Teacup and miniature dogs may be more prone to broken bones.

With that in mind, let's discuss any differences regarding miniature, toy, and teacup variations of the Boston Terrier. According to the American Kennel Club, these variations are not recognized as acceptable by Club standards. Often, these words are interchangeable – they are all used to describe a "runt" puppy (or the offspring of two runts) that is being passed off as a novelty item (therefore drawing a larger price). Most experts simply suggest avoiding getting a Boston Terrier that is smaller than the accepted standards as they experience many health problems. As a pet parent, I can personally tell you that once you become attached to a pup, whether he lives a few months or for twelve years, you will be heartbroken should he succumb to health problems. Save yourself the heartache – get a standard sized Boston Terrier from a reputable breeder.

Some dishonest breeders will breed these smaller dogs knowing that they may experience more health issues compared to standard-sized dogs. Some may also practice inbreeding to achieve a very small dog. Others may deliberately underfeed a puppy in order to stunt its growth. Each of these practices can lead to health problems for your future pup.

Should I Consider Cheap Boston Terriers for Sale?

Again, use the same caution that you would with any breeder. Ask questions. Ask for a health guarantee. Use your intuition regarding any breeder. Breeders who do all that they can to promote the health of their dogs often invest a good bit of money into food, vet checks, and general care. Vet care expenses for the parents, particularly the dam, can add up quickly. This care doesn't end once the puppies have been born. Some breeders take the puppies in for check-ups multiple times before offering them for sale. In addition, a reputable breeder will have ensured that the puppies have had at least one round of vaccinations. Sometimes they will pay for an initial worming treatment (most puppies regardless of the cleanliness of a breeding facility are born with roundworms; a general first vet visit includes a "de-worming" treatment). If the vet has to perform any genetic testing, this expense can drive up the cost of your pup. You can combat this by asking to look at health records for the puppies and the parents. Just keep the old adage, "You get what you pay for," in mind.

Where Can I Find AKC Registered Puppies?

Most breeders with registered dogs do so through the American Kennel Club. However, there is another registration organization in the United States, the Continental Kennel Club. Some breeders look down on the CKC because they do not have the same standards as the American Kennel Club. However, as you contact the breeder, inquire about registration. The American Kennel Club website provides resources on AKC-registered pups for sale.

Is There a Special Price for Female Boston Terriers?

Often, yes, there is a higher price for female Boston Terriers compared to a male Boston. This may include full (unlimited) registration rights so that you can breed the female later should you choose to do so. Also, females are often in greater demand than male puppies, so breeders may feel more comfortable asking a higher price for a female puppy. Often, there is no set price for male versus female pups. This is up to the discretion of the breeder. Some breeders charge the same amount for either gender; others charge a higher price for females. There is nothing set in stone that says you will definitely pay a higher price for a female Boston Terrier puppy.

Where Can I Find a List of Boston Terrier Breeders Near Me?

First, ask for recommendations from people you trust. Let a search of the Internet or the classified ads be your last resort. Also, consult the Trusted List in the Bonus chapter. If you know someone who breeds a different type of dog, ask that person about reputable Boston Terrier breeders. In addition, the Boston Terrier Club of America has a list of reputable breeders on their website (http://www.bostonterrierclubofamerica.org).

Figure 9: A Boston Terrier with her pup

CHAPTER 4

Should I Consider Adopting a Boston?

As I mentioned in the previous chapter, I recently obtained an older female Boston that I believe might have come from a puppy mill. While I did not technically adopt her, my experience with her is similar to what many face when adopting an older dog. I would recommend adopting a Boston of any age, simply because Bostons do tend to bond to their owners, no matter their age. However, adoption is not for everyone, particularly those with little experience with dogs. You may need to exhibit more patience with an older dog than with a puppy. However, keep in mind that an adopted dog seems to know that you rescued him or her from a sad life, and they seem even more devoted than the average Boston. For that reason alone, yes, I highly recommend adopting a Boston Terrier.

Should I Consider an Older Boston Terrier?

Absolutely! Shelters and rescues are full of older Boston Terriers. Often, people do not want to adopt an older Boston Terrier; they opt for a younger pup. However, the Boston will bond to its new owners just as a young dog. Some owners swear that the older dog "knows" that you rescued him from an unhappy situation, and he may be even more devoted to you.

However, you need to consider that the older Boston Terrier may have some behavioral issues that stem from his life prior to coming to the rescue. Although there are some owner surrenders (such as an older person with health problems that prevent him from caring properly for a dog), not every situation is ideal. You may have to work to gain the trust of an older Boston Terrier that has had a difficult life. However, within a short period of time, your Boston will acclimate to life with a good owner, and you will enjoy the benefits of a relationship with an awesome dog.

How Do I Find a Boston Terrier Rescue?

Often, you can do a simple Google search to find nearby Boston Terrier Rescues. One great place to start is the Boston Terrier Rescue Net website (https://www.bostonrescue.net). This website lists rescues throughout North America, including Canada. While not all states are home to a Boston Terrier rescue facility, it is possible that a neighboring state does house a Boston rescue.

Be prepared to fill out an ample amount of paperwork at a Boston Terrier Rescue facility. Like a reputable breeder, they want to see the dogs go to good homes. Also, expect to pay almost as much as you would for a puppy (approximately $450.00; different facilities will have varying prices for adoption. This usually includes any medical treatments, spay/neuter of the dog, etc.).

What Types of Boston Terrier Rescues are Available in Florida?

The Boston Terrier Rescue of Florida is centrally located in Lake Mary, Florida; however, they also have several satellite facilities. Often, a person can view their available dogs on Petfinder.com, or the interested individual can view them via the Boston Terrier Rescue of Florida website.

The Boston Terrier Rescue of Florida accepts surrendered animals, and they have a very extensive application process. Potential adoptive parents can expect to fill out an application and pay a non-refundable fee to begin the process. Some of the dogs available are considered senior dogs (age six and older,) or are special needs. If you are interested in a dog of this type, you may be able to be matched with a dog within a few months. However, if you want a younger dog with no health issues, you may wait a year or longer to bring home a furry friend. Often, potential adoptees go through the approval process before a dog is even available for adoption. Potential adoptive pet parents will need to provide veterinary references, as well as fit other criteria. Often, Boston Terrier Rescue volunteers will contact a potential adoptee via telephone to review the application and complete that part of the adoption process. Next, the Boston Terrier Rescue of Florida will visit your home to make sure that it is safe for a Boston. Once this part of the process has been completed and approved, you will begin the waiting process for a dog.

The fee for adopting a Boston from this rescue range from $200 - $600, depending on the age and health of the dog.

Each dog adopted out of the Boston Terrier Rescue of Florida is microchipped, spayed or neutered, and up-to-date on shots and heartworm treatments. These expenses are included in your adoption fee.

What Types of Boston Terrier Rescues are Available in Texas?

Texas is home to multiple Boston Terrier rescue facilities. One is located in North Texas; the other has multiple locations, often partnering with PetSmart stores to sponsor adoption events. As with the Boston Terrier rescue facility in Florida, you will need to fill out an adoption application and pay a processing fee. The North Texas Boston Terrier Rescue serves the entire state of Texas. It is an all-volunteer organization much like that of the Florida facility. To find out more information about the exact adoption process, adoption fees and what is included in your adoption fee, contact the North Texas Boston Terrier Rescue (https://www.texasbostons.com).

Where Can I Find Reputable Boston Terrier Rescues Near Me?

The Boston Terrier Rescue Net website has links to reputable Boston Terrier rescues throughout the United States and Canada. (https://www.bostonrescue.net)

CHAPTER 5

What Can I Expect When Living with a Boston Terrier?

What is the General Temperament of a Boston Terrier?

The Boston Terrier is a friendly, loyal, stubborn, loud, mischievous, and sweet little dog. He never meets a stranger, and he makes friends easily. The Boston Terrier is never shy. A Boston Terrier bonds to his family rather quickly and some Bostons suffer from separation anxiety if their owners spend a good deal of time away from home. The Boston does crave attention, and you should be careful not to allow him to develop small dog syndrome.

Small dog syndrome is a behavioral issue in many varieties of small breeds. To be sure, it is not the fault of the dog – its origins lie in the relationship a pup has with his pet parent. Small dog syndrome occurs when a dog is allowed to "take over" – he may disobey the rules, bark incessantly, and nip at strangers. In other words, the small dog thinks that he is "boss" – and the owner simply allows him to get away with bad behavior. Should you notice this type of behavior in your Boston Terrier, you must become firm and consistent in correcting him. Like other terriers, the Boston needs a "pack leader." This means that he *must* see you as his "alpha," or lead" dog. You, the pet parent, must be in control, and you must expect your dog to be on his best behavior. Much like a small child, the Boston Terrier must have limits and discipline. This may sound harsh, but, in the long run, the Boston Terrier will actually be a better dog in the end. On a positive note, not all Boston Terriers (or other small dog breeds) will develop small dog syndrome. Lay a firm foundation in how you train him and stay consistent. You and your Boston will be happier in the long run.

The Boston Terrier is a very energetic little dog. However, as hard as he plays, he naps just as hard. The Boston is rarely aggressive, but I have witnessed some Bostons getting upset during a verbal spar between two members of his family. I have even witnessed a Boston get between a father and son as they tussled and rough-housed. Some Bostons may become upset when a parent disciplines a child. This leads to the next point of interest . . .

Is the Boston Terrier Good with Kids?

In my experience, the answer is a resounding YES! When both my children were small, our Bostons were always curious about the new infant (and, truthfully, they were a tad jealous); however, no Boston I have ever owned has attempted to nip at or bite either of my children. Remember, the Boston is not an aggressive breed. He will defend himself if necessary, but even then, he has to be prodded.

Figure 10: A child at play with her Boston Terrier;
Boston Terriers and children get along very well.

Bostons seem to have an instinctual bond with kids. However, remember, if you do not have children, always find opportunities for your Boston baby to socialize with kids. This will acclimate them, and the Boston will learn what type of behavior you expect from him at all times.

Boston Terrier Behavior

In describing Boston Terrier behavior, let me ask you to imagine a very mischievous child or a mischievous family member. This impish little fellow also has the ability to look at you and make you forgive his misbehavior. The Boston has so many positive qualities all wrapped into one package!

He is a very loving breed; when I say that he does not meet a stranger, he rarely does. "Shy" is not a word in his vocabulary. He enjoys any attention he may receive from house guests; if you have him out and about in the neighborhood, he will enjoy stopping to greet people right along with you. (NOTE: In a previous section, I mentioned the possibility of small dog syndrome. Often, dogs with this behavioral issue will not warm up to guests. This is NOT normal Boston Terrier behavior, and you should take note as to other unwanted social habits.)

Always one for extra attention, you might consider training him not to jump up on people from a young age. Although this is only his way of saying hello, your neighbors might not appreciate his friendly mannerisms. He is also likely to greet any guests at your home in the same manner that you do. Unfortunately, the Boston Terrier is prone to mouthiness (lots of barking). Some owners describe their Boston's propensity for barking in this manner – "if he hears a leaf fall outside, he's going to bark at it." Unfortunately, this is true, but, you can look at this as the idea that the Boston is a great watchdog.

If you believe that excessive barking will be an issue for you, then focus on teaching him to be quiet. When he starts to bark, use the word "quiet." When he stops barking, praise him and give him a treat. Of course, you will need to repeat this several times in order to get him to understand what you expect of him. Some people advocate using a collar to correct this issue. However, since the Boston Terrier is prone to issues such as narrow airways and a collapsed trachea, I do not recommend a shock collar. The method I proposed above can be time-consuming, but, for health reasons, steer clear of a collar for training your pup to be quiet.

The Boston Terrier can be somewhat hyper at times, but, within thirty minutes, the Boston is likely to be napping away. The Boston Terrier is also prone to stubbornness, so training will require persistence and patience. However, his stubbornness is not of significant proportions, and he is generally easy to work with. Down deep, the Boston Terrier wants nothing more than to please his owner. He is deeply bonded to his family, and he is attuned to their moods. Owners often admit that a Boston seems to know when he has misbehaved, and he may hide from you when he thinks he might be in trouble. Overall, the Boston Terrier is truly a joy to own. His loving, friendly personality makes it difficult not to like him.

Figure 11: The Boston is happiest when spending time with his owner.

What is to be Expected from a Boston Terrier's Health?

The Boston Terrier is generally a healthy small dog; however, there are some health issues that the Boston is prone to. This is why is it is so important to seek out reputable breeders when purchasing a Boston. A Boston Terrier generally lives between twelve and fifteen years. One should be sure to give the Boston proper exercise as he can become inactive indoors and put on weight. In the previous chapter, I mentioned choosing a reputable breeder to ensure that your new Boston is as healthy as possible. While I will discuss choosing a breeder in future sections, I do want to mention a few things to look for when visiting potential breeders. First, look at the facilities. Multiple dogs outside in cages is rarely a good sign when visiting a breeder.

The deadly Parvovirus can live on the ground even through extreme temperatures, so there is no guarantee a new puppy has not been exposed to the deadly disease. Moreover, the general goal of a puppy mill is to mass-produce dogs for a profit. Some irresponsible breeders are not careful in their breeding practices; this means there could be inbreeding in the facility or there could be other dishonorable breeding traditions within the puppy mill, such as breeding a female over and over again with no regard for her health. Either of these practices can contribute to the health of your new puppy. First, inbreeding in Boston Terriers can cause minor problems such as dental issues, or it can be fatal in a puppy. Repeated breeding of a dog can cause a depletion of the natural vitamins and minerals of the body. The immunity of the dog may also be compromised, and this can have an adverse effect on the health of a puppy. So, what does a puppy mill or puppy farm look like? First, wire cages with no solid flooring on the bottom are stacked on top of one another. Next, the facility will not be sanitary. Often, sellers who will not allow you on their premises do so because their facilities might be considered a puppy mill or otherwise disreputable. If you suspect that the facility you are visiting is a puppy mill, then ask the breeder for a health guarantee regarding the puppy. Consider it a significant warning signal if the breeder refuses to allow you onto his or her property; generally, reputable breeders have no problem allowing potential buyers to tour their facilities. If the breeder refuses to agree to such a condition, then you should look elsewhere for a new puppy. Further discussion of reputable breeders will be discussed later in the book.

Do Boston Terriers Experience a lot of Health Problems?

The Boston Terrier is generally a very healthy, hardy little dog. He does experience some health issues no matter how healthy he is, but simple TLC can keep these issues from affecting his quality of life.

In a previous section, I discussed the brachycephalic nature of the snout of the Boston Terrier. Here, I'd like to explain that a little further. Brachycephalic is the medical term used to describe the short, flat faces of many breeds including the Boston Terrier (other brachycephalic breeds include the Lhasa Apso, Pug, and Pekingese). These dogs have a short muzzle, which, in effect, is situated in their throats (in comparison, to a Collie, whose snout is long). The skull of a brachycephalic dog is often compact as well. In addition, the airways of the flat-faced dog are generally narrow (remember, it is basically down the throat of the dog). The respiratory system may also be compact. Part of life with a Boston Terrier often involves listening to them snore, snort, or wheeze. Some brachycephalic dogs are also prone to reverse sneezing (often compared to a wheezing sound; reverse sneezing often takes place when the dog is excited and may be the result of allergies). Reverse sneezing is not harmful to the dog, although it may sound terrible.

Now that you understand what the term brachycephalic means, let's further explore the ramifications of this type of health issue, and what you should do to take care of your Boston Terrier. First, always outfit your Boston with a harness for exercise purposes rather than a collar. A harness will distribute the pressure of the leash/harness combo evenly across the already-compromised chest area. Using an elevated bowl for food and water for your Boston will keep him from inadvertently inhaling food or water into his lungs. In the previous chapter, I briefly discussed keeping your pup from getting overheated or overexerted. Most dogs should be given physical activity at times of the day when it is cool, but, for the brachycephalic dog, exercising early in the morning and later in the evening is imperative. A brachycephalic dog already has difficulty breathing in ideal situations, but when he is outdoors – particularly in humid climates and especially during warmer months – breathing for the brachycephalic dog is highly difficult. When walking the Boston Terrier, it is a good idea to carry water with you so that he does not become overheated. While panting works to cool off a dog with a "normal" snout, the narrow passages of the brachycephalic dog do not draw enough air to cool the dog properly. In addition, the extra stress on the dog's already compromised respiratory system can cause heart problems – particularly cardiac arrest. Overexertion presents the same problems that overheating does. Some experts advise treating a brachycephalic dog much like you would an asthmatic child – do not expose them to extreme temperatures, high wind, or high humidity.

Some brachycephalic dogs are prone to dental issues due to the fact that their teeth are often crowded. The Boston Terrier generally does not suffer from crowded teeth, but he usually has a significant underbite as a result of his facial structure. Some pups that are inbred may have teeth that protrude from the lips. (This is particularly found in red Boston Terriers, who have been subjected to inbreeding.)

Again, the Boston Terrier is a relatively healthy dog. However, he is prone to some health issues just as any other dog. In particular, the Boston Terrier may experience eye issues such as cataracts or a condition known as cherry eye, a condition in which an inner portion of the eyelid flips over and bulges out from the lower inside corner. He may have some joint issues such as patellar luxation, a type of knee dislocation in which the patella moves out of place. Deafness is an issue that many Bostons face. Boston Terriers may also face serious issues such as brain tumors, and they are prone to allergies as well.

Some Boston Terriers experience a disorder known as megaesophagus. This condition results in the regurgitation of undigested food. Megaesophagus differs in conventional vomiting in that the food comes back up without warning. Dogs often hack before they vomit. Your vet may need to treat this defect in the esophagus.

Let's discuss the other health issues a Boston might face. Cataracts in dogs are much like cataracts in a human. A filmy piece of tissue appears over the lens of the eye, making vision difficult. While cataracts can appear in many dog breeds, the Boston Terrier is prone to juvenile cataracts. This form of the condition presents itself when the dog is a mere eight to twelve weeks. Many experts stress requesting a guarantee of eye health before purchasing a new puppy. While adult cataracts can be surgically treated, a veterinary ophthalmologist should be consulted in order to treat juvenile cataracts, which are often invisible to the naked eye.

Cherry eye affects many small dog breeds, including the Boston Terrier. Cherry eye takes place when a gland located in the third eyelid prolapses. Cherry eye can be treated with surgery.

Patellar luxation is also known as "slipped stifles." Simply put, the patella, or kneecap, becomes dislocated due to the fact that the femur, patella, and tibia bones are maligned. This can be quite painful for the affected dog, and, left untreated, can eventually lead to arthritis. Patellar luxation has varying degrees of severity, and the most severe cases may need to be surgically corrected.

Bostons may also be affected by heart murmurs, which are highly treatable and do not take away from the quality of life of the dog. Your vet will often prescribe a reduced sodium diet, an exercise plan, and diuretics to prevent an enlarged heart.

Figure 12: A Boston Terrier with one white ear and a blue eye

Be careful about choosing a Boston Terrier that has a white head (or at least one-third of his head, including the ears, is white). Often, a dog with a white head and white ears will also be deaf. Sometimes, this dog will also have one or both blue eye(s). Somehow, genetically, this combination predisposes them to deafness. While deafness does not restrict the quality of life of the affected pup, it can place restrictions on the things he can do. I have a deaf Boston, and she is generally a happy dog. She suffers from separation anxiety, which is partially something a Boston is prone to, but I believe that having her "people" near give her a sense of security. Deaf Bostons can be trained with hand signals, but a deaf dog will need to be accompanied outside at all times. He should never be allowed outside unless he is leashed, or he is inside an enclosed area. Training may be a little bit more difficult with a deaf Boston, and training may take a little longer when compared to a hearing dog. However, have no fear – a deaf Boston will learn what you want from him, you just have to take a different approach. We personally used hand signals with our deaf Boston.

Some Boston Terriers, like many other breeds, may develop brain tumors.

A common ailment for many Boston Terriers is allergies, both the kind affecting the digestive system and those affecting the skin. Often, both varieties of allergies present the same type of symptoms. You may notice your dog scratching at his ears and face. Swelling may be present in his face as well. To prevent food sensitivities and possible food allergies, always feed your dog a diet that has little or no artificial coloring or preservatives and does not contain grains such as corn. In addition to scratching his face and ears, you may also notice his hair coming out in patches. Again, switching his diet to one that contains no wheat or corn (and you may have to introduce a gluten-free food) will help to resolve these issues.

Pointers on Choosing Boston Terrier Food for Puppies

Making sure that your Boston Terrier puppy gets proper nutrition as he or she is growing is imperative to keeping your dog healthy for a lifetime.

Puppy food is specifically formulated to deliver twice the nutrients present in typical adult dog food. As puppies grow, their rapidly developing bones and muscles crave protein first and foremost. A good puppy food will contain no less than thirty percent protein in addition to a balance of certain vitamins and minerals, particularly vitamin A, B, C, D, E, and K. The puppy food you choose should contain fats and carbohydrates as well.

Learn at this point in your dog's life to read the nutritional labels provided. Two things you will want to see on the label are the words "balanced" and "AAFCO approved." First, the government requires dog food companies to ensure that both puppy and adult food is nutritionally balanced. However, the term "AAFCO approved" is not required of dog food companies, but it can mean the difference between quality food for your pup and cheaper food rife with fillers and little nutritional value.

AAFCO stands for Association of American Feed Control Officials. This group sets a certain standard for animal food, and labels which contain this distinction are exceeding typical food guidelines. You will not find artificial preservatives and fillers in foods with this label. This is especially important to Boston Terriers, who can often experience food allergies (particularly to grains such as corn). Other Bostons may experience digestive issues which also necessitate a healthier diet. By purchasing dog food with the AAFCO label, you can ensure that your dog is getting top nutrition.

Ingredients that you should most definitely avoid include grains and preservatives. Look for terms such as corn or wheat gluten, meat/grain meal, meat by-products, BHA, BHT, Ethoxyquin, dyes such as Blue 2, Red 40, Yellow 5 and/or 6, and 4-MIE. Yellow 5 has been found to be particularly dangerous to dogs of any breed. Propylene Glycol and rendered fat are two other terms to avoid when choosing dog food.

Many dogs have difficulty processing corn; like humans, dogs can have corn allergies which can cause issues with their coat, such as hair loss or intense itching. Dogs, like humans, may also have issues with gluten.

Meal and meat by-products – if a label reads lamb meat by-products, this can mean that any part of the lamb was in effect ground up and added to the ingredients of your dog's food. Often, "meal" by-products are *bone* meal – a ground bone placed in your dog's food. This can be difficult to digest and has little nutritional value. It is merely a filler and can have negative effects on your dog's digestive system. Meat by-products are the parts of a slaughtered animal not approved for human consumption and can include anything from the intestines of an animal to the brains or kidneys. Another food label you should search for is "pet grade." If you see the term "feed grade," then the quality of the nutrition is low.

It is tempting to forgo feeding your new Boston Terrier puppy food; however, as puppies develop, the higher concentration of vitamins and minerals present in puppy food give your dog proper nutrition without extra calories. Also, remember that the most expensive puppy food is not the best-suited dog food for your pup. Read the label, look for AAFCO approval, and ensure that the food you choose is packed with protein, vitamins, and minerals rather than grains.

Many of these ingredient do's and don'ts are also applicable to adult Boston Terrier dog food.

What Should I Consider when Choosing Food for Adult Boston Terrier Dogs?

Figure 13: Boston Terriers love meal time!

My objective herein is not to convince you to choose a certain brand of dog food, but to encourage you to carefully read the labels of a variety of dog food offerings and make the best choice for your dog. Many Boston Terriers can eat most any brand of food as long as it is nutritionally balanced. Never let anyone convince you that unless your dog is eating highly expensive food that you are doing your dog a disservice. On a personal note, after doing a good bit of research, I purchased some fairly expensive dog food. It fit all the criteria – organic, nutritionally balanced, AAFCO approved – but my dogs hated it. They might eat half their allotted portion. I share that experience to assure you that you will need to experiment and find the right food just for your dog. The price that you pay for dog food is not exemplary of the love you have for Fido.

First, remember the same instructions when reading the ingredients. Look for the terms "balanced" and "AAFCO approved" first and foremost. Next, look for those ingredients that are to be avoided: meal by-products, meat by-products, certain color additives (yellow and blue color additives, to be sure), BHA and BHT, feed – grade quality, Ethoxyquin, and Propylene Glycol. No matter if your dog has no other health issues, these preservatives and additives can cause great harm to your Boston and should be avoided.

Why are these ingredients so harmful, and, if they are, why would companies include them in food for pets? To be honest, these ingredients are inexpensive. Keep in mind that pet food companies are not subject to the same scrutiny as those who sell human food. However, once again, do not let this fool you into believing that the most expensive dog food is the best food for your Boston. Generally, dog food with a middle-of-the-road cost is the best food – both nutritionally, and for your pocketbook as well.

So, just exactly what are these additives? What can they do to my Boston? First, let's look at the color additives. Blue 2, Red 40, and Yellow (5 and 6) have all been linked to allergic reactions, and, even worse, cancer. There is really no reason to have a color additive in pet food – remember, your dog is color-blind, and he has no preference for a particular color in his food.

BHA stands for Butylated Hydroxyanisole. It is a chemical preservative found in both pet food, and some pet treats. Both BHA and BHT (Butylated Hydroxytoluene), as well as Ethoxyquin, are known to cause cancer in lab rats. You might be surprised to learn that Ethoxyquin is illegal for use in human foods, but not in pet foods. NOTE: Often Ethoxyquin is NOT printed on the food label. It is masqueraded as *fish meal*. By law, a food label – whether it be located on dog food or on human food – cannot make false claims. Therefore, always look for the statement "no artificial preservatives" on your dog's food label. This will guarantee that none of the aforementioned chemicals are present in your pooch's provisions.

Propylene Glycol is a moistening agent present in many soft dog foods. Unfortunately, Propylene Glycol is a derivative of antifreeze, a known toxin.

Now that you know what to avoid when choosing a dog food, one should consider what ingredients are necessary for the health of your Boston. As previously stated, vitamins such as A, B, C, D,

E, and K should be a part of the food you choose for your Boston. Should you be located in the United States, search for the phrase "Made in the U.S.A." on the label as well. This guarantees that the food manufacturer will have to follow FDA standards for pet-grade food. Speaking of the grade of food, ensure that your dog's food is labeled "pet-grade" rather than "feed-grade" food.

As your dog grows, you may notice some digestive issues affecting your Boston. According to the American Kennel Club, certain symptoms will manifest denoting either a sensitivity to a certain food or a full-blown food allergy. Food sensitivities often appear even after your dog has eaten a certain food a number of times. You may notice vomiting and diarrhea twelve to twenty-four hours after eating the offending foodstuffs. The dog's coat will often be affected – you may notice frequent itching or whelps on the skin. These symptoms may or may not be coupled with chronic bacterial infections.

It is important to note that often, food sensitivities are mistaken for food allergies. However, the sensitivity generally builds up over time, and it will disappear as soon as the offending food is removed from the dog's diet. Surprisingly, a real food allergy is rare in a dog. The major difference in food sensitivities and food allergies is that there is an immunological response to the offending food, such as anaphylactic shock one might experience after eating peanuts. The response will be almost immediate. Another allergic reaction to food involves breaking out in hives and/or facial swelling. This will not be immediate but will manifest within a short time of consumption (two to four hours).

If you find that your dog does have a food intolerance, there are foods on the market that you can try before purchasing a vet-prescribed food. First, many dogs with sensitivities and allergies have difficulties digesting certain proteins. Therefore, their diet should be modified so that the offending protein – generally dairy and wheat proteins are the culprits – is removed. Hypoallergenic dog foods are those that contain venison, duck, and salmon as a protein source. They may also replace wheat with potatoes or peas. This is called introducing a "novel" protein into the dog's diet to see via trial and error if beef and wheat proteins are causing the allergic reaction in your dog. Most experts recommend feeding a hypoallergenic diet for two to three months while assessing your dog's response to the new food. Often, within six weeks, you will see an improvement in your dog if food sensitivities and allergies prove to be an issue for your pup.

The Boston Terrier is known to be sensitive to certain foods. You may notice patches of missing hair, facial swelling, or excessive itching. You will notice him scratching his ears incessantly if he is being affected by digestive issues. Introducing the hypoallergenic diet should relieve much of his irritation, return his coat to its beautiful sheen, and make life in general much more enjoyable for your Boston. However, keep in mind that you may have to enlist your veterinarian in eliminating certain foods from your Boston Terrier's diet. You may end up with prescription dog food. Note your dog's symptoms and keep a log of his diet.

What is the Best Food for Boston Terrier Adults?

Speaking of food sensitivities, the best prevention for allergic reactions or other food sensitivities is to provide the best possible food in the first place. What constitutes the best food for an adult Boston Terrier? Consider the ideas discussed in chapter three. Read labels and look for labels which state that the food meets AAFCO standards. Of course, one major decision you need to consider is wet versus dry dog food.

Wet dog food contains a greater amount of moisture than dry kibble, and this can be beneficial if your dog does not drink a great deal of water. This type of dog food also contains contrasting nutrients that your dog needs – high protein and virtually no carbohydrates. Wet dog food rarely contains artificial preservatives because the can is sealed. It is more appealing to your dog, and dogs with a finicky appetite will often eat wet dog food when they eat nothing else. Wet dog food is actually a great choice for smaller dogs because it is easier to chew.

Dry dog food is not nearly as palatable as canned dog food; often, manufacturers will add gravy or other fats to increase the appeal of dry kibble. It does not provide much moisture, and, if your dog does not drink properly, he may experience kidney issues. Dry food is often high in carbohydrates, and not necessarily the good grains either. Dry kibble may not provide an adequate amount of healthy fats or carbohydrates for your dog, particularly if he is very active.

Of course, when looking at these issues, one would think that wet dog food would win out as the best dog food for a Boston. However, one must keep in mind that wet dog food as a solitary source of sustenance will lead to a soft stool, and wet food can promote weight gain when compared to a diet of dry kibble.

In addition, wet dog food is much more expensive than its dry counterpart.

One area that should be explored is cooking your own dog food. Consider the ingredients in the dry kibble which is AAFCO approved for small dogs: chicken, lamb, or fish, rice, peas or carrots, and sweet potatoes. Some brands also use pumpkin as a healthy carbohydrate. These things can be prepared in your own kitchen for roughly the same price as a sixteen-pound bag of dry kibble. First, choose the type of meat you wish to prepare. (When I prepare meals for my dogs, I generally choose chicken. Lamb is not readily available in my area, and I am allergic to fish, so I can't handle it.) Beef is also a great alternative to these meats. (TIP: Choose stir fry beef or stew meat as these are lean cuts.) Ground chuck is not a very good choice unless you get the lowest choice of fat possible. Boil the meat, seasoning it only with a minimum amount of salt (sea salt is recommended). White rice is a "novel" grain that does not have the same possible allergic reaction as corn or wheat. To make things easier, you can add canned carrots, diced potatoes, green beans, and peas (you can find these in the organic section of your grocery store). Depending on the amount of rice you cook, this amount of food (roughly three pounds of meat, four cups of rice, and the vegetables) will yield a week's worth of food for slightly less than a bag of dry kibble. In addition, you know exactly what ingredients are in your dog's food. Plus, your dog will be so excited to eat "human" food. I have been feeding my dogs this type of diet, and I have seen distinctive improvements in their behavior and coat. One of my Bostons would often scratch his ears until he whined. He no longer scratches at his face. I have noticed less gas – almost a given when living with Bostons – and rarely do I notice a loose stool.

All in all, the best choice of Boston dog food is up to you, the pet parent. You may face trial and error in finding the perfect food for your pooch. Remember, consider what the dog enjoys eating, look for signs of food sensitivities (remember – an allergic reaction is immediate whereas a food sensitivity seems to be a progressive issue). Always read your product labels and make an educated choice for you and your Boston baby.

What is the Best Food for Boston Terrier Puppies?

Choosing a nutritional food for your growing puppy is just as important as choosing a proper food for your adult Boston. The first twelve months of any breed of dog's life are crucially important to their overall health as an adult dog, Like our own children, Boston puppies need certain nutrients in just the right amount in order to grow into healthy adult dogs.

Figure 14: The Boston Terrier puppy needs special nutrients to grow properly.

Again, utilize the puppy food label to determine if it is a good choice for your Boston baby. Just like with adult dog food, you will want to avoid artificial preservatives and colors. Steer clear of foods that include the terms "meal" – as in bone meal, blood meal, and so on. Walk away from foods with the terms "animal by-product" on the label. Again, these are not true meats; these are often products that are derived from the carcasses of slaughtered animals. Should you notice these terms at the head of the list of ingredients, you should most definitely put that bag of dog food down and move on. These products are never healthy for your dog at any age.

Now that you know what to look for when discarding potential dog food choices for your Boston, let's focus on ingredients that you DO want to see included in your puppy's food.

First, look for ingredients that promote healthy brain development. One prominent ingredient in a nutritionally-packed dog food is DHA omega fatty acids. Not only do DHA omega fatty acids encourage healthy brain development, but they also promote healthy skin and eyes.

Some puppy foods also include probiotics. Taking in healthy probiotics at such a young age actually helps build a healthier digestive system for your Boston Terrier. Keep in mind that some Bostons have issues with food sensitivities. Feeding them probiotics may help eliminate some of these sensitivities and other digestive issues such as regurgitation.

Some puppy foods also have a higher amount of protein formulated in their product as well as healthy carbohydrates.

Puppies do need a higher amount of these nutrients compared to adults, in order to meet their energy needs.

Still, other puppy foods include ingredients such as L-carnitine, EPA omega-3 fatty acids, fiber, and whole grains. Fiber aids in digestion, as does the use of whole grains rather than starchy carbohydrates. EPA omega-3 fatty acids and L-carnitine aid in healthy skin and eye development. While these ingredients are highly beneficial to your Boston baby, they are not non-negotiable. At a minimum, you should ensure that your puppy's food includes DHA fatty acids, probiotics, and plenty of protein and healthy carbohydrates.

Previously, I discussed cooking a healthy meal for your Boston Terrier adult. Unless you are able to include the same ingredients as listed above, it is a wise investment to find a suitable commercially-made puppy food. Ensure that the puppy food is geared for small breeds; the kibble will be smaller and easier to chew.

Dry puppy food is recommended for puppies aged ten to twelve weeks up to their first birthday. What should you do in the meantime? At one time, breeders would wean the puppies and have them ready for their forever homes at six weeks. Today, the trend is moving toward waiting until the puppy is eight weeks old before taking him completely away from his mother. Often, the mother will begin to wean the puppies at four to five weeks. At this time, the breeder will generally begin switching the pup to traditional puppy food. Often this includes soft dog food. Some recommend "soaked" dog food. Simply add water to the dry kibble (puppy food) that you have purchased. Do not pour the water off – the puppy will drink it as well. All this does is soften the kibble for puppies with developing teeth.

You will need to feed your eight to twelve-week-old puppy four meals a day. He will need about 400 calories a day. When your puppy reaches three months of age, reduce his feedings to three meals a day. You can continue to "soak" his food at this time. Once he is four months old, you can begin reducing the amount of water in his food. At six months of age, you can put him on a schedule of two meals a day. He should be fed twice a day, to ensure the proper number of calories throughout the day. Remember that he should have special puppy formulated food, for the first twelve months of his life.

What About Treats for my Boston Terrier?

Using treats in training your Boston pup is almost imperative, so I would be remiss if I did not add some pointers on choosing a proper healthy treat for your new companion.

First, you will want to consider the number of calories in a treat. Bostons only need between 300 and 600 calories per day as an adult, so experts recommend that only ten percent of this amount come from treats. For this reason, you will want to stick with small treats that do not contain many calories. Consider that your dog should not take in more than seventy calories from treats on a daily basis. A good average would be twenty calories or less per treat. (There are some treats available that have less than five calories per piece.)

Next, treats should be soft and tasty. Be sure that the treats do not contain any of the artificial additives (such as BHA or Ethoxyquin) that have been mentioned previously in this chapter.

If you live in the United States, you may also look for other labels such as "Made in the USA" which denotes that the treat is made to conform to FDA standards.

Remember, small, tasty, and soft treats with low calories are perfect for training your Boston baby.

CHAPTER 6

What are Some Health Issues the Boston Terrier Experiences?

What is Special about the Boston Terrier Muzzle?

The Boston Terrier is referred to as a brachycephalic breed. In essence, his airways are narrower due to the fact that his nose is short. Compare the Boston Terrier to a Collie. The Collie has a long, normal muzzle for a dog. His airways are not compressed. They have ample room to do their job. If you think about it, in some ways, the Boston is built in a way that his airways aren't outside his face in the muzzle, but partially in his throat. As discussed previously in the chapter, the Boston can become overexerted, and, while he does pant in order to cool off, you must remember that the Boston's airways are compromised by their narrowness and location. It is for this reason that experts recommend elevated bowls as well. Compare it to your attempting to eat when you have a cold, and your nasal passages are blocked. Like other dogs, the Boston can become enthusiastic about his food, and he may seem to "inhale" it. When using a regular bowl, he can become strangled during enthusiastically eating. The elevated bowl puts the Boston in a position in which his airways are more open.

Do Boston Terriers Suffer from Allergies?

Yes. Like other breeds, the Boston is prone to food sensitivities, and he can be sensitive to allergens in the air just as we humans can.

As previously stated, a Boston with a food sensitivity will often experience hair loss. In my experience, the hair will come out in a circular fashion. It is often a little larger than the size of a quarter. The dog will scratch at the area. He may also scratch at his face or ears. One of my male Boston Terriers would scratch his ears until he whined. I switched his diet, and he immediately stopped the scratching/whining cycle. Other dogs will experience ear infections due to a food sensitivity.

Although many Boston Terrier pet parents will laugh about the fact that their Boston baby is rather gassy, this characteristic is actually a possible food sensitivity symptom. Boston Terriers do have a sensitive stomach, and they do experience a good bit of flatulence even when eating the healthiest diet. However, if you notice more frequent gassiness in addition to regurgitation and/or diarrhea, then you may need to change your dog's diet. He could be experiencing a food sensitivity.

Boston Terriers can also suffer from allergies involving reactions to dust and pollen (similar to that in humans). His eyes may be watery, and he may produce an abundance of mucus. Experts recommend adding omega fatty acids to your

Boston's diet in order to help alleviate some of the irritation of environmental allergies.

Also, keep in mind that your Boston may have sensitive skin, so be careful in selecting a shampoo for him. Do not be tempted to use human shampoo on your Boston. He can develop hives in reaction to even the gentlest human shampoo. Chapter 8 goes into great detail regarding the selection of shampoos for your Boston.

What is the Boston Terrier's Life Expectancy?

The Boston Terrier generally lives for twelve to fifteen years. In my personal experience, my Bostons have lived for eleven or twelve years on average. However, many factors go into the health of your dog. Providing him with healthy food when he is a puppy, getting regular physical examinations, and regular heartworm treatments can add years to the life of your beloved Boston.

CHAPTER 7

Should I Breed my Boston?

First and foremost, let me say that time and time again, dogs who have been spayed and neutered tend to live longer than an intact male or female. For instance, certain types of cancers can be avoided in addition to other reproductive organ issues. Even if you do decide to breed your Boston, after one or two litters, you should consider spaying or neutering your dog for their overall health.

Do you love your Boston so much that you'd love to have a puppy like him or her? Keep in mind that extra-special care must be taken when breeding a Boston Terrier female. Also, your Boston Terrier female may need to undergo a C-section in order to birth the pups, due to their abnormally large heads. However, this is not always a given. You will need to be available to sit with your Boston as she gives birth in case a trip to the vet for surgery is necessary. Also, keep in mind that most females who undergo a C-section will be spayed at the same time.

All females should be allowed to go through at least two "seasons" or "heats" before breeding is even considered. Experts recommend waiting until at least the second birthday of the female to even think about breeding. If so, you will have allowed her to build up the proper amount of nutrients in her body so that the pups will be as healthy as possible.

Figure 15: Very young Boston Terrier puppies

Some breeders mix puppy kibble in with the regular dog food that their females eat, in order to provide the pups with optimum nutrition even before they are born. This is a smart idea, and it can only benefit your pups. Breeders may introduce the mixture of puppy kibble once the mom has given birth. There is no wrong time to introduce the nutrients that puppy food can provide. The extra vitamins in the omega fatty acids and protein will help build up both the mom and her pups.

Also, keep in mind the size of the dogs you intend to breed. A very small female (about fifteen pounds) should not be matched with a large male (twenty-five pounds). This could increase the likelihood of complications during delivery.

It is also a good idea to get a physical exam for your female, prior to breeding. Make sure all vaccinations are up-to-date and make sure that she is not suffering from any health issues.

CHAPTER 8

What can I Expect When Training my Boston Terrier?

The Boston Terrier has two attributes that will aid you in training: high intelligence, and a willingness to please his owner. Conversely, the Boston Terrier also possesses one detrimental personality characteristic that may make housebreaking and other training endeavors slightly difficult – he can be rather stubborn at times! However, two things are key on the part of you, the trainer: patience and persistence.

Is Boston Terrier puppy training difficult?

Let me say from personal experience, that the Boston Terrier is not a difficult breed to train. However, I learned quite a bit between the first pair of Bostons I owned and the second pair that I currently own. Consistency and a rewards system will aid you in successfully training your Boston puppy. You have to remember that he truly wants to please you, and he can sense when you are upset with him. Never punish him for accidents that he has in the house. Instead, reward him with healthy treats when he does a good job. He will learn much more quickly than you realize.

Expect to be up and down at night with a Boston baby for the first two weeks of its life in your home. After that, his bathroom schedule will become more routine and not as frequent. However, there is a way to combat this issue as well. It is a combination of crate training with puppy pad training, and it is likely this is how your Boston will come to you (using puppy pads in the crate with his mom). (Puppy pads are made from cotton encased in a protective material which serves as a barrier between the cotton and your floor.) With my first pair of Boston babies, I would take them outside each time they woke from a nap or ate a meal. I am not exaggerating when I say I have literally picked up a pup the moment he began stirring after a nap to take him outside to the bathroom. I realized the folly in this as I grew older. Never let your puppy touch the ground outside until he has had at least the second set of vaccinations. Why? Unfortunately, parvovirus – a highly contagious illness that often comes on rapidly and is usually fatal if not treated in time – lives on the ground through all types of weather. Yes, parvovirus can live through extreme heat and cold, even when the ground is frozen. I was fortunate that my first Boston puppies did not contract parvovirus, and I do not recommend ever taking a puppy out until it is at least nine weeks old AND he has had the second set of shots. So, that brings us to crate training.

As much as those big brown eyes will pull at your heartstrings, it is best if you purchase a crate for your dog to sleep in. You can also begin training him with puppy pads at this point. Place his bed in one corner of the crate, and line the bottom of the crate with a puppy pad. (Hint: Puppy pads are often scented with pheromones that prompt the puppy to use the pad. This will help as you move him outside the crate for housebreaking.) Dogs will not lie where they have used the bathroom, and, although he may have a few accidents, he will often go to a corner of the puppy pad to eliminate waste, without getting any on his bed. Once you bring him home, you will want to make sure he has a fresh puppy pad in his crate at all times. He cannot hold his waste at such a young age, but this will improve within just a few weeks. While it is tempting to hold him at all times while he naps, allow him to take some naps in the crate. He will learn that he should use the puppy pad when he needs to go, and, at this point, you can begin placing the puppy pad in a place that you want him to go (for example, in the utility room). I recommend taking him to the puppy pad after each feeding. If he uses the puppy pad successfully, reward him with a treat. He will pick up on the idea that you want him to use the puppy pad placed in that area. This will help to keep accidents to a minimum when the weather is bad, and you can't take him outside.

Again, I recommend training him to go outside to the bathroom after the second round of shots, usually at eight weeks. My youngest Boston Terrier was purchased during the winter, and because of the bitter cold, I chose not to train her for outdoor bathroom duty until she was closer to three months old, when the weather began to warm up. To be honest, she took to using the bathroom outdoors much more easily than my previous dogs. I attribute this to her being more mature at the time I began training her to go outside to potty. You will find if you wait just two or three more weeks (until your puppy is about three months old) – and, granted, puppy pad training is messy at best – you will complete potty training much more quickly and successfully than if you push training on your pup before he or she is ready.

When training your dog to go outside to use the bathroom, again, taking him or her upon waking from a nap and after every meal, is a good start. Be prepared to wait a while at first. It may take several attempts before your puppy understands he is outside for a purpose, not just for play. You may find yourself outside with him for a half hour at a time. However, always have a treat handy when he is successful. Even at three months, your puppy will remember that he gets a reward for doing something that comes naturally. He will also begin to notice that he does NOT get a treat when he has an accident indoors. By reinforcing good behavior – using the puppy pad and using the bathroom outdoors when the time is right – he will learn what you expect of him.

You should expect the Boston to have accidents off and on during his first nine months, especially. Often, Boston Terriers are not fully housebroken until they reach one year of age. However, by the time he is six months old, he will be in a routine, and his accidents will be only minimal. Remember to take him out to use the bathroom at roughly the same time every day. I have had more than one Boston who would go and sit at the door, then turn his head to look back at me as if to say, "It's time to go out!" Always remember to heap praises on him for a job well done, and he will be trained much more quickly than he would with negative reinforcements.

I also recommend leash training at the same time as housebreaking. Again, do not take him outdoors until he has had preventative vaccinations. Set him down, and begin to walk, calling to your pup to follow. Leash training is very easy, and I highly recommend beginning around three to four months old. Often, the dog does not mind the leash and will learn to stop and go as you tell him. However, some Bostons could rival a Siberian Husky pulling a sled in the Iditarod. (And don't be fooled – even at fifteen pounds, that puppy is stronger than you think!) You must take time to teach him or her to heel to your command so that you don't get pulled down. Leash training should begin at an early age. Often, older dogs who are not used to wearing a harness and a leash will fight them.

Figure 16: A Boston Terrier wearing a harness

Should I Consider Harness Training my Boston Terrier?

Considering that the Boston Terrier has a predisposition to developing a collapsed trachea, I absolutely recommend harness training for your dog. A harness discourages a puppy who likes to pull. Harnesses put an equal amount of pressure across the chest area, and dogs who are trained using a harness are more focused. It is an effective training tool as well; however, a front-clip harness is best for controlling your dog. As with potty training, begin getting your dog accustomed to a harness as quickly as possible. You can put your puppy in a harness from day one.

Do Boston Terriers require a carrier or cage?

I am a firm believer in crate training a Boston, particularly due to the fact that many Bostons exhibit separation anxiety. The Boston Terrier experiencing this behavioral problem will often find relief in the coziness of a crate or cage. I personally use the wire crate (which might appear to be a cage at first glance). The exact measurements are described in chapter 9. As previously stated, you can place your Boston's bed, a toy, even a water bowl in his crate. Over time, your dog will find his crate a secure place. Of course, especially when your Boston Terrier is young, do NOT put him in his crate as a punishment. You may notice your Boston putting himself in his crate during times that might be upsetting to him, such as during a thunderstorm. (My deaf Boston will take her nose, open her crate door, and get inside her crate, especially when my other Bostons are roughhousing, which she doesn't care to take part in.)

CHAPTER 9

How do I Prepare my Boston Terrier for Crate Training?

First, you will want to introduce your puppy to the crate. Keep in mind that your puppy is already experiencing a lot of "firsts" during his initial time with you, and he may whine, or act upset, in the beginning. So, you will need to make sure the puppy associates the crate with something pleasant, such as a treat. With a small puppy, you may have to place him in his crate for a few weeks. This will actually help him acclimate to crate training. However, if your puppy is a little older, you may need to coax him into the crate by placing treats outside the crate, with a few inside as well. Another way to help your puppy see the crate as a pleasant place is to feed him inside the crate. If your puppy walks willingly into the crate, then place his dish at the far side of the crate. If not, place the food bowl just inside the crate. As he begins to enter the crate more on his own, make a point to move his bowl a little further back in the crate until he enters the crate with no problems. It is important at this time that you keep the door closed. You may have to start out with leaving him in the crate for three to five minutes each day, increasing the time he is inside the crate after a meal until he is staying in the crate without a fuss for at least ten minutes. Never allow your puppy out of the crate when he is whining; in fact, you are teaching him that all he needs to do is whimper, and he will be released from the crate. Again, NEVER, ever use the crate as a punishment tool.

Once your dog stays in his crate without whining for at least ten minutes, then you can start lengthening the time that your pup stays in the crate. When your puppy enters the crate willingly, give him a treat. Be sure to give him plenty of praise.

Once you are sure that your puppy is comfortable inside the crate, then you can begin to leave the room for five to ten minutes at a time. Consider this a test run on how he will behave if you have to be away for a few hours at a time. After that short time period, come back to the room, sit down beside his cage and talk to him in a calm manner. Wait a few minutes, then let him out. Give him a treat and heap praise on him. He will learn that he can stay by himself for a short time and that his person will always come back to him.

A few pointers – never leave your dog crated for a majority of the day and night. Your dog needs proper exercise, and, most of all, he craves time with you. Should a puppy be left in his crate for hours upon hours, he will come to resent the crate. The crate should be used for potty training in his early months, and to aid an insecure puppy dealing with separation anxiety. The crate should not be the primary residence of the dog.

Another pointer – I have mentioned the wire crate that I tend to favor. I've included a picture of the crate that I use. Notice that this crate has a removable tray at the bottom of the structure.

Figure 17: This crate features a removable tray for easy cleaning.

This tray is invaluable when you are potty training your pup. You can remove the tray, a dirty puppy pad, and you can rinse off any soiled areas. Also, even though puppy pads are designed to absorb urine, sometimes there is just going to be run-off. Notice that the tray has sides which will prevent any urine from pooling and running off into the floor.

Another thing I like about this crate is the fact that your dog will not feel so closed in (as opposed to using a plastic crate that is more enclosed). He will still be able to see you. If you are concerned that your pup might get cold inside this crate, then you can purchase a cloth crate cover. Just remember – make the crate a pleasant experience for your dog, and he will adjust to crate time.

Pointers on Boston Terrier Dog Crates

One thing you should be aware of is the idea that many Bostons suffer from separation anxiety. In fact, I personally owned a Boston who would become destructive if I left her even for an hour at home alone. Actually, I once left to run a quick errand and found my kitchen littered with garbage upon my return. It was at this point that I became a firm believer in using a crate. My Bostons nap in their crates; I leave a toy and a fleece blanket in their crates, and they feel secure should I have to be away from home for an hour or two. (With that said, no dog should ever be left in a crate for more than a few hours at a time; that is not the recommendation. The small space of the crate gives the dog a sense of security. The crate should never be a means of punishment either; I will address crate training later in the book.)

Because your Boston is not a large dog, you do not need to purchase a large crate for him. In fact, a medium-sized crate (30 in. x 19 in. x 21 in or 76.2 cm x 48.26 cm x 53.34 cm) is often the perfect size for your Boston. (Some crates are 36 in x 19 in x 21 in (or 91.44 cm x 48.26 cm x 53.34 cm); this is totally acceptable as well. I don't recommend going much bigger as this will not help out with separation anxiety.) NOTE: Some experts recommend a cloth covering which covers three sides of your crate for added snugness and security. This is not necessary. Much depends on personal preference and the severity of your dog's separation anxiety.

CHAPTER 10

What are Boston Terrier Standards and Most Common Colors?

T he Boston Terrier Club of America is the authority on the breed standards regarding the Boston. According to the written standard, "The Boston Terrier is a lively, highly intelligent, smooth-coated, short-headed, compactly-built, short-tailed, well-balanced dog -- brindle, seal, or black in color and evenly marked with white. The head is in proportion to the size of the dog."

The weight of the Boston is divided into three classes by the Boston Terrier Club: first, under fifteen pounds; second, fifteen to twenty pounds; and third, twenty to twenty-five pounds. A Boston's leg length must be proportional to the length of the body; in addition, the bones and muscles of the Boston must be in proportion to the body. A "blocky" or "chunky" Boston does not fit the breed's standard.

The head of the Boston must also conform to certain features in order to be considered the traditional Boston skull. The skull is often squared, the top flat as well as the cheeks; its stop is well-defined. Eyes are wide apart, set square with the skull, and outside corners of the eyes appear to be in line with the cheeks. The ears are small and erect; they are set in the corners of the flat-topped skull. Some describe the ears as almost bat-like. The muzzle of the Boston is of great importance – it is short, square, and is in proportion to the dog's square skull. According to the standard, a Boston's muzzle will not exceed a length which is one-third the length of the skull. It should also be parallel to the top of the skull. A Boston's jaw is square, and the teeth are short, otherwise regular. Often the bite will be somewhat undershot. The tongue or teeth may not show when the mouth is closed.

Figure 18: The Boston Terrier's nose is considered brachycephalic

The neck of a Boston is in proportion to the rest of his body. The back is short and appears to "square" the body. The topline (the topline of a dog is a line straight down the middle of the dog's back, starting between its shoulders and ending at its tail) should be level. His rear will curve slightly. His tail is short, often a "corkscrew," but it may also be straight. It must be fine and taper at the end regardless of other characteristics.

The shoulders of a Boston are sloping and laid back. Elbows stand in line with the rest of the leg, neither appearing to stand in or out. Forelegs are set evenly apart, in line with the shoulders. Feet are small and round. Thighs are muscular; the hock joint is well-defined, and the hocks themselves turn neither in nor out.

A Boston's gait is sure-footed. The Boston is often quite agile. He seems to move in a perfect rhythm. Words like "graceful" and "powerful" often describe the movements of the Boston. His feet should never cross as a part of normal movement.

His coat will be short and smooth. A Boston should never have lengthy or silky hair.

The Boston, according to breed standards, is either brindle, black, or seal in color with white markings. These white markings appear on the muzzle band, a white blaze between the eyes down to the muzzle, and a white forechest. Often, he will also have white on his forelegs and hind legs (the appearance of white "socks").

Figure 19: This Boston has the traditional black and white markings.

Black Boston Terrier

The typical Boston terrier is black with white markings as described above. An all-black Boston Terrier does not follow the standards set forth by the Boston Terrier Club of America.

White Boston Terrier

An all-white Boston Terrier does not conform to the standards set forth by the BCTA. As this is not a typical color for the Boston, some inbreeding may be practiced in order to keep the white color prevalent in a litter. An irregular bite is often evidence of this inbreeding.

Gray Boston Terrier

Figure 20: This Boston is considered gray. Some also classify him as silver or blue. This does not conform to AKC breed standards.

The gray Boston is not so much an issue of improper breeding as it is a genetic mutation; therefore, the gray Boston does not have the health issues of a Boston who is specifically bred to be white or red. According to experts, the color gray is a "dilution" of the traditional black coat; "this dilution is due to a mutation of the dilution gene which is Chromosome 25, in canines." Most breeders simply use parents who share this mutation of the gene; repeated inbreeding is not necessary to produce the gray coat.

Figure 21: This red Boston Terrier does not conform to breed standards.

Red Boston Terriers

Red Boston Terriers are not approved under the standards of the American Kennel Club or the BTCA; however, the red Boston is the most recognized color variation. According to some breeders, the red color is considered a mutation (much like the gray Boston coloring). However, some disreputable breeders will inbreed two red Bostons, in order to continue the coloration. Some breeders advertise the red Boston as a "rare" color, and they may charge a higher price for this. Be sure to check for signs of repetitive inbreeding – such as a severe underbite or other dental issues – before purchasing a red Boston.

Figure 22: This is a brindle Boston. Notice the streaks of color in his coat.

Brindle Boston Terriers

The Brindle Boston Terrier is a variation of coloring that is accepted by the American Kennel Club; however, the brindle Boston should have the characteristic white markings on his face and chest, similar to the black Boston Terrier.

Red and White Boston Terriers

Please see "Red Boston Terrier" for more information about this color variation of the Boston.

Tan Boston Terriers

The tan Boston Terrier is yet another disallowed color (non-standard). Some experts believe that somewhere in the lineage of a tan Boston, a Boxer has been introduced. Many times, the tan Boston will appear to have a "mask" much like the markings of a

Boxer. In addition, this color is often the result of interbreeding a Pug and a Boston Terrier.

Figure 23: This Boston can be considered a "blue" Boston due to its light coloring.

Blue Boston Terriers

The blue Boston Terrier is a variation of the gray Boston Terrier. The only variation is the terminology in which breeders use to describe the coloration.

Brown Boston Terriers

The brown Boston Terrier may also be referred to as a liver-colored Boston. It is also not approved as a standard color for the Boston Terrier. Often, the brown Boston will have one blue eye or both eyes will be blue in color, which is a disqualifying physical characteristic according to the American Kennel Club and the Boston Terrier Club of America.

Seal Boston Terriers

*Figure 24: A Boston Terrier with a seal coat.
Notice how the red hue shines through his coat.*

The seal Boston Terrier often appears to look no different than the black Boston Terrier; however, in the sun, the seal Boston will appear to have a reddish cast to his coat. The seal Boston Terrier color is acceptable under both American Kennel Club and Boston Terrier Club of America standards.

Other Issues in Breed Standards

Some Bostons, particularly the red variation, may also possess one or both blue eyes. Not only does this variation disqualify a Boston from recognized breed standards, but it also presents some health issues for the affected pup. Often, a dog with blue eyes may be deaf. This is particularly true if the dog has predominantly white ears. Other disqualifying characteristics which prevent a Boston Terrier from meeting AKC/BTCA standards also include eyes that show too much white, splayed feet, a sway back, a Dudley nose (one that is pink in color), and a wry mouth. While none of these characteristics make a Boston Terrier a lesser dog, pups presenting these disqualifying characteristics will not be allowed in the show ring. However, if you simply want a sweet dog who is a great companion, color variations with no other physical defects do not interfere with the pleasing personality of a Boston.

Figure 25: This white-headed Boston does not meet breed standards.

Because Boston Terriers are so intelligent, should you happen to procure a Boston that happens to be deaf, he or she can be trained to learn hand signals. However, a deaf Boston Terrier can never be left unattended outside. He should be leashed trained, and he should never be allowed to run free unless he is in an enclosure. Otherwise, he can live just as full a life as a Boston with full hearing capabilities.

What is Involved in Showing Boston Terriers?

First, your Boston must be at least six months old. Males may not be neutered, and females may not be spayed. You must ensure that your pup fits all the breed standards outlined previously (no Dudley nose, color patterns, eye color, etc.). The American Kennel Club recommends becoming a member of local dog clubs (the AKC website provides links to clubs), as well as taking classes to learn what is expected of you and your dog during a dog show. You may show your dog yourself, or you may hire a professional to do so. When you are ready to enter shows, be sure that each show provides qualifying points in the event you are interested in participating in at AKC title shows. Most experts recommend attending a few local shows to get an idea of what showing a dog requires. Showing your dog can be a rewarding experience for the both of you and being a part of these showing events will widen your circle of trusted Boston Terrier owners.

CHAPTER 11

What Items Will I Need in Order to Care for my Boston Terrier?

T he Boston is not a high maintenance dog. He does not shed heavily. His hair is short and straight, and owners can generally brush him every two to four weeks to ensure that dead hair and dander does not end up on the family's furniture and clothing. The Boston can go for two to three months without a bath; in fact, it is probably best to use an all-natural dry shampoo on your Boston baby. However, choosing the right food for your Boston is extremely important. Some Boston Terriers require a special diet due to digestive issues or allergies. Let's address the type of diet that your Boston will need from puppy to adulthood.

Boston Terrier Bedding

Most often, your Boston will wish to sleep cuddled next to you on your bed. However, this is not always a good habit to promote in your dog.

Small dogs in particular need a bed that is cozy, makes them feel safe and will keep them warm. A nest bed is a perfect bed for a small dog such as the Boston Terrier. To make sure that you are purchasing just the right size bed for your Boston, consider your dogs' size when he stretches out. The bed should be just big enough so that he will not slide off the bed when he stretches. The great thing about a nest bed is the fact that it has raised sides – these sides both promote warmth for your dog and also lend to a feeling of coziness.

Should your Boston be subject to allergies, be sure to avoid certain fillers in the dog bed – such as cedar. In addition, you can purchase a hypoallergenic cover for your dog bed to prevent any allergic reactions.

Vaccinations

The exact vaccinations your Boston will be required by law to undergo will vary according to your location. At six weeks, your puppy will receive his first round of immunizations. At this time, he will likely be given shots against distemper, kennel cough, and parvovirus. You may see the term "bordetella" on the list of vaccinations – this is the prevention against kennel cough, a highly contagious respiratory disease among canines.

At twelve weeks, you will return to the vet for another round of vaccinations. These include the second immunization against distemper, parvovirus, and bordetella. In addition, a vaccination for infectious hepatitis will be administered at this time.

At fourteen weeks, the third booster for parvovirus and distemper will be administered. A second immunization for infectious hepatitis will be given, and you will have the option to also vaccinate against Lyme disease and leptospirosis.

At sixteen weeks, the last round of shots for your pup's first year will be administered. Parvovirus and rabies are the required shots at this time, and you will have the option to add leptospirosis and Lyme disease as well.

At one year, you will return for booster shots. This includes a final parvovirus immunization as well as a final administering of the distemper and infectious hepatitis immunizations. A final rabies booster will be given as well. Pet parents have the option also to administer the bordetella immunization a last time, as well as a parainfluenza, leptospirosis, and Lyme disease vaccination.

You can expect yearly boosters for kennel cough, leptospirosis, parainfluenza, and rabies.

Schedule of vaccinations through the first year

Average Age at Vaccine Administration	Vaccines Administered
Six Weeks	Distemper Bordetella Parvovirus
Twelve Weeks	Distemper Bordetella Parvovirus Infectious Hepatitis

Average Age at Vaccine Administration	Vaccines Administered
Fourteen Weeks	Parvovirus booster Distemper booster Infectious Hepatitis * Lyme disease * Leptospirosis * This denotes these are optional vaccinations.
Sixteen Weeks	Parvovirus booster Rabies * Lyme disease * Leptospirosis * This denotes that these are optional vaccinations.
One Year	Boosters for all previous vaccinations

Some pet parents opt not to give their dogs vaccines; however, you should keep in mind that most states require at the very least a rabies vaccination. Some cities require pet parents to register their dogs and to provide proof of rabies vaccinations. Also, keep in mind, at some point you may need to board your dog. If so, you will need documentation of the bordetella immunization. While kennel cough is rarely fatal, it can rob your dog of some of his quality of life, and you may not be able to board him should you find yourself needing to be away overnight.

Another bit of preventative medicine that you should always be aware of is heartworm prevention. Heartworms are transmitted via mosquito bites, and, if your dog will be outside at any time, it is vitally important that your dog receive preventative heartworm medication. Many times, a dog does not show symptoms of a heartworm manifestation until the problem has become life-threatening. Conversely, some dogs with a severe infestation may experience lung damage from medications used to treat such cases of heartworms. Therefore, prevention is key to the health of your dog. While heartworm cases have been documented in all fifty states, states along the Gulf Coast, the Mississippi and Ohio Rivers, and the Eastern Seaboard tend to have a higher incidence in heartworm cases.

Boston Terrier Gear

So, we have looked at Boston Terrier bedding and food, but what are some other items that are necessary for your Boston's health and well-being?

Boston Terrier Dog Bowls

First, let's think about the feed and watering bowl you will need for your Boston. Earlier in the book, the brachycephalic snout of the Boston Terrier was discussed. While we know that it does affect the activity level of the Boston, does this require a special type of dog bowl for the Boston Terrier? The answer is an unequivocal yes. In fact, you will also need to keep this in mind when purchasing leashes and harnesses for the Boston. First, we will look at the type of feeding and watering bowls that are best for the Boston.

The flat face and brachycephalic snout of the Boston are adorable, but it also presents issues for the dog where breathing is concerned. Even at rest, the Boston tends to snore, snort, and possibly wheeze. Because of this, the Boston requires an elevated bowl for both feeding and water. It is never a good idea for a brachycephalic dog to have to eat with his head downward, and elevated bowls will keep the Boston from choking as he eats.

Boston Terrier Collar/Leash/Harness

Again, this is an area where you will need to consider the idea that the Boston Terrier is a brachycephalic dog. Often dogs with the short snouts common to brachycephalic syndrome are prone to a condition known as a collapsed trachea. Also known as a windpipe collapse, a collapsed trachea occurs when the cartilage rings in the windpipe weaken and become misshapen. This can cause breathing difficulties due to obstructions in the trachea. Tracheal collapse is often a hereditary condition, and it is more prominent in small dogs such as the Boston Terrier. For this reason, it is highly recommended that you forgo a collar for walking your Boston, and, instead, invest in a harness. Over time, pulling on the throat of your Boston with a collar and leash can contribute to a collapsed trachea (and, unfortunately, some Bostons will pull at their collars with the strength of a sled dog). Using a harness for walking your Boston will allow for more equal distribution of pressure as you walk your dog. A harness causes no respiratory distress in your dog and is better for him overall. This is not to say that you can't put a decorative collar on your Boston – for instance, to put his name tag – but a harness is better for use when walking your Boston Terrier.

Boston Terrier Clothing

Figure 26: Some Boston pet parents enjoy dressing their pups.

Boston Terriers do not have a double-coat, so, if you happen to live in a cooler climate, you may want to invest in some clothing for your Boston baby. However, this is a personal preference. I only dress my Boston Terriers on occasion, and they seem annoyed with it. However, likely they are "annoyed" because it is not something that they are accustomed to. Had I made their wearing clothes a habit, they would likely take wearing clothing with the usual laid-back attitude of the Boston.

Boston Terrier Toys

The Boston Terrier has a propensity for chewing – chewing shoes, chewing some pieces of furniture, even chewing his dog bowl! For this reason, providing your Boston with proper chewing toys is always beneficial to preventing the destruction of your property. Again, the brachycephalic nature of the Boston's snout plays a part in the product you should choose for your Boston Terrier. Avoid rawhides – this includes pig ears and bully sticks. Often, a Boston will chew this until it becomes like play-doh, and they can swallow this. At times, the rawhide itself is not dangerous to the dog, but, if he swallows a good-sized portion of the rawhide, it may simply gag him and come right back up. A great all-natural chew toy is the cow hoof. The cow hoof is good for the teeth. It disintegrates on its own, and it will never choke the dog. Some cow hooves have a barbeque flavoring added; however, most dogs prefer them as chew toys, regardless of extra flavors. In addition, low-cost cow hoof lasts much longer than rawhide.

Be careful when choosing rubber toys for your Boston. Although he may not appear to be so, your Boston Terrier is a chewing machine. A rubber toy that is not well-made can break apart, and, if your Boston swallows this material, it could cause serious damage.

CHAPTER 12

What Other Issues Should I Consider When Purchasing a Boston Terrier?

Boston Terrier Items

Your Boston will not require a large number of items to be a happy, healthy pup. A dog bed, healthy chew toys, and a dog sweater should you live in cooler climates, are the most important items to purchase when you bring your Boston baby home. The Boston is a happy, laid-back dog that does not require a lot of maintenance. He is happiest when receiving attention from you.

Harness vs. Collar

Previously in the chapter, we discussed using a harness versus a collar with the Boston Terrier. I have used both a collar and a harness with my Bostons over the years. While I have been lucky in that using a collar did not result in a collapsed trachea in one of my first Bostons, I have used a harness with my current pups, and the benefits are visible. I have one Boston female who loves to pull while on her leash. The harness prevents her from pulling away. The harness promotes an equal distribution of pressure on her chest. As one dog expert puts it, collars are for dog tags (identification), and harnesses are for walking with the leash.

Keep in mind that a collapsed trachea might not become symptomatic until a dog is considered "middle aged" – four to six years old. By then, the damage has been done. Sometimes a collapsed trachea requires surgery to repair the damage. Considering that an ounce of prevention is worth a pound of cure, it is best to forgo a collar and stick with a harness when it comes to using a leash.

Boston Terrier Dog Toys

Also discussed previously in the chapter, I am a huge proponent of the cow hoof all-natural chew as a toy for your Boston Terrier. Never give your Boston rawhide chews. There are appropriate rubber toys that you can give your Boston; however, be aware of cheaply made toys as they can tear and be swallowed by the pup. I have used tennis balls from the sporting goods section of the store as a dog toy, but, these can also become punctured by the dog. A good idea is to watch your dog's toys. If you notice the toy developing holes or the hide becoming torn, it is best just to throw it away. Another great toy for your Boston is a rope-type chew toy. Some are knotted at both ends; others may have a tennis ball threaded onto the rope so that you can play tug-of-war with your pup. On a personal note, this is one toy that I highly recommend based on the desire of your Boston to spend time with you. The Boston prefers games such as fetch and tug-of-war, all of which are interactive.

Boston Terrier Shampoo

Boston Terriers are often plagued with dry skin. They do not have an undercoat, and their fur is usually short and somewhat coarse. Some experts recommend only bathing the Boston once or twice a month. Others recommend only bathing your pup when he is dirty, such as after playing outside (Bostons do enjoy rolling in mud or dirt while playing outside).

Bostons often develop whelps or bumps on their backs. These are often in response to a strong shampoo (a skin sensitivity). Some owners use baby shampoo on their pups. I advocate an all-natural shampoo. Now, keep in mind that many manufacturers will slap "natural" on the label of their shampoos, but there are still additives in the product. Unfortunately, only a certain amount of ingredients need to be present in order for a manufacturer to be legally able to put this label on a pet product. For most dog product manufacturers, the terms "natural" and "organic" are merely marketing tools – and the general public does not know the difference. Again, this is where you need to be able to read the label to decipher the ingredients listed. Terms such as "proprietary blend" and "naturally derived" are tell-tale signs that the product in your hand is *not* all natural. In fact, often this signifies that the manufacturer only added a few natural ingredients – or a watered-down version of the natural (or organic) ingredients – and then sends the product on to you. Next, look at the product itself. If it is thick, it is likely that additives have been included in the shampoo to make it appear more like the traditional shampoo we are accustomed to. To know for certain, look for the additive guar gum on the label. Another easy-to-spot sign that a dog shampoo is not all natural

is the color. Truly natural dog shampoo looks like cooking oil –
it is not very thick and is often yellow in color. If it is any other
color, the manufacturer has likely added artificial color to the
shampoo. Natural colorants which have been approved for human
consumption are rarely found in dog shampoos, so keep that in
mind if you happen upon an all-natural shampoo that is a bright
(unnatural) color. Also, don't be afraid to open up the bottle and
smell the product. If the product has a strong, distinct smell, it
is likely due to artificial fragrances added to the product. Often,
the label will only read "fragrances," and this is because, in order
to achieve a certain smell, many ingredients (often toxic to dogs)
must be combined in order to produce that fragrance. By law, the
manufacturer is not compelled to list what ingredients have been
added to achieve a particular fragrance. In order to be certain that
you have purchased a safe dog shampoo, look for this phrase on
the label – "certified organic." Products labeled USDA Certified
Organic must meet certain guidelines, and artificial fragrances
and colors are not allowed in these products. You may spend a
little more to purchase this type of shampoo, but it is well worth
preventing skin issues and possibly severe illnesses that can come
with using products containing artificial ingredients.

What is the Best Boston Terrier Brush?

A natural bristle brush is the best type of brush for a Boston
Terrier. Keep in mind that the brush needs to be soft. A Boston
Terrier's coat is thin, and a coarse brush could cause him
discomfort. Also, use a gentle hand when brushing him. He will
only need to be brushed once every week. Some Boston owners
prefer to use a hound's glove (a hound's glove is basically a
mitt which has special grooves that act as massaging tips), as it

mimics the act of simply petting your dog. The hound's glove also promotes the distribution of natural oils throughout the dog's coat, which will leave him looking shiny and healthy.

What Boston Terrier Accessories will I Need?

Boston Terrier Dog Coat – Bostons living in cooler climates will appreciate a dog coat during the winter months. The Boston's coat is very thin, and while you may choose to use it only when walking outdoors, it may benefit your Boston to use it indoors as well (particularly if you keep the temperature rather low in your home).

Figure 27: Bostons living in colder climates will need proper clothing.

Boston Terrier Chew Toys – Avoid rawhides and cheaply made rubber toys. Tennis balls are acceptable toys; but throw the ball away should you notice the hide beginning to come off. Rope-pull toys are a good choice for the Boston, as is the cow hoof.

Figure 28: A Boston Terrier puppy at play

Boston Terrier Gear – The Boston does not require a lot of gear or accessories to be happy. An elevated bowl, a harness, a dog sweater for cooler months, and a few healthy chew toys will keep the Boston happy and healthy.

Boston Terrier Dog Collar – The Boston Terrier should only wear a collar for the purpose of displaying his name tag. His collar should be loose enough so that you can comfortably place your finger between his neck and the collar. Keep in mind that the Boston Terrier can develop a collapsed trachea as a result of wearing a collar that is too tight or from wearing a collar and using a leash on the collar. Use the harness for the leash when exercising outdoors.

Boston Terrier Dog Leash – A four to six-foot nylon leash is best for training a Boston Terrier. You may also choose a leash of the same length made from leather; it is also durable and will not break. There are leashes made of cotton and rubber, but don't be tempted to purchase them – they are not as durable as they'd seem. Keep in mind that Bostons tend to pull, and a short leash helps in preventing some of this behavior. I personally do not recommend a retractable leash for a Boston Terrier. Often the material is just not as durable as that of a nylon leash. You can also get rope burns from a retractable leash should you have the misfortune of getting your hand or fingers caught in the line when your Boston pulls forward.

Dogs can also become strangled should they pull too much line, that doesn't readily retract.

A six-foot line (1.8228 meters) is the length that I recommend using; I find that I have more control with this length. Combine this leash with a front-clipping harness, and you will have ample control over your Boston baby.

Boston Terrier Dog Bowl – An elevated dog bowl is necessary for your Boston Terrier. Also known as an elevated feeder, this bowl helps you Boston to maintain good posture in addition to minimizing choking during feeding. Some experts also believe that using the elevated feeder will help decrease the trademark gassiness of the Boston Terrier. You will not need to elevate the feed and water bowls very high for your Boston; often just elevating his feeder just a few inches off the floor will help open up his airways, so that he can eat and drink comfortably.

Boston Terrier Dog Bed – I like to imagine that if a Boston Terrier could be questioned as to what type of bed he enjoys the most, he would likely say that he prefers to sleep in the bed with his owner! This is a decision you will have to make. Studies show that dog owners who allow their dog to sleep with them, often experience a more disturbed sleep experience. Also, consider the fact that you may have to be away overnight from time to time, and this may have an adverse effect on your dog's ability to rest while you're away. A dog bed with raised sides or even a "cave" style bed will work well for your Boston Terrier baby. Many Boston babies enjoy burrowing down in the bed, and these types of beds provide this opportunity.

CHAPTER 13

What are Some Examples of Boston Terrier Mixes?

B eginning in the 1980s, people began experimenting with designer breeds. Truthfully, this is a purposeful mixing of two purebred dogs. Some dogs, such as the Maltipoo and Goldendoodle, are still very popular today. In fact, some breeders work with designer breeds exclusively. Some designer breeds are second and third-generation dogs (meaning their parents are also the mixed breed, not two purebreds matched together). These so-called designer breeds often have their own personalities and health issues aside from that of the original breeds. However, use the same caution you would when choosing a purebred Boston Terrier breeder. Below a few of the most common Boston Terrier mixed breeds.

Boston Terrier Chihuahua Mix

The Boston Terrier and Chihuahua mix is commonly known as either the "Bo-Chi" or the "Boston Huahua." The Bo-Chi has a short, dense, silky coat. His exact coloring will depend on the parents, but he may be black and white, cream, (all) white, brindle, or brown and white. He is the size of a toy dog, weighing anywhere from six to fifteen pounds. Again, his exact size will depend upon the dominant parent breed. Unlike the purebred

Boston Terrier, he is not good with children or with other pets. This is due to the fact that the Chihuahua is often a "one person" dog. The Bo-Chi is known to be hypoallergenic, which is a great point if you tend to have seasonal or environmental allergies. He is also generally highly alert and energetic. He is highly protective, and the Bo-Chi makes a great watchdog.

He will not need a great deal of exercise, just a short walk twice a day. He is usually an active indoor dog. Supply him with a variety of toys, and the Bo-Chi will get adequate exercise just by playing normally.

The Bo-Chi will not be as easy to train as his Boston Terrier parent. Unfortunately, the Chihuahua parent can be slightly stubborn at times, and this trait may present itself in the Bo-Chi. However, take the same approach as you would with the Boston Terrier. Use treats and praise to reward good behavior, and the Bo-Chi will soon learn what you expect of him.

Boston Terrier Pug Mix

The Boston Terrier Pug Mix is an adorable designer breed. Sometimes referred to as a "Bugg," the Boston Terrier-Pug mix often has the best characteristics of both breeds.

Because the Pug and the Boston Terrier both have a brachycephalic snout, you can also expect to see this trait passed on to the Bugg. However, the Bugg is not as prone to his eyes popping out of the socket, as the purebred Pug.

The Bugg lives an average of ten to thirteen years. This might be considered somewhat exceptional as most designer breeds do not live as long as their purebred counterparts.

The Bugg can live anywhere – a home with or without a fenced in yard or an apartment of any size will suit the Bugg. He generally weighs between fifteen and twenty-five pounds, and his height varies, depending upon the dominant parent breed.

It is easy to determine the temperament of a Bugg; the Boston Terrier and the Pug already feature similar temperaments. They are very affectionate with anyone they meet, but particularly with their pet parents. They love to play, and the especially get along well with children. However, the Bugg may inherit a propensity for becoming territorial with his "person." If so, this behavior should be corrected as soon as possible, as it is highly negative. Treat this behavior as you would "small dog syndrome" behavior. Establish firm rules, and make sure that your pup knows you are "the boss."

Remember that the Bugg will be a brachycephalic dog; he will have the same issues with overheating, eating, and narrow airways as the Boston Terrier or Pug parent.

The Bugg can be a variety of colors – brown, black, or white. Again, this will depend on the dominant parent breed.

Boston Terrier Bulldog Mix

The Boston Terrier Bulldog Mix is often known as the English Boston-Bulldog. Much like the Bugg, these breeds are already quite similar, and they tend to do well when bred together.

The English Boston-Bulldog is not a highly active dog. He will enjoy two or three brisk walks around the neighborhood. He will likely be brachycephalic also, and so you will need to take care when allowing him to exercise. He should not be allowed to get too hot or to become overexerted as he will have the same breathing issues as a Boston Terrier (an English Bulldog may also experience brachycephalic syndrome, like the Boston and the Pug).

The English Boston-Bulldog is wonderful with children, protective of them, and loyal to a fault. He is known to be very affectionate with kids and playing with children ranks high on his list of hobbies.

The English Boston-Bulldog will have a short, fine coat that does not require much in the way of grooming. As he may experience some of the same skin issues as a Boston Terrier, it is best to provide him with the same type of diet as discussed in this book. You should also use an all-natural shampoo on the English Boston-Bulldog.

The English Boston-Bulldog will be bigger than the Boston Terrier. He will weigh about forty pounds, and he will be about sixteen inches in height. His exact size, however, will depend on the dominant parent breed.

The English Boston-Bulldog has a life expectancy of nine to twelve years.

Figure 29: A Boglen (Boston Terrier/Beagle mix)

Boston Terrier Beagle Mix

The Boston Terrier Beagle mix is commonly known as a Boglen Terrier. He is larger than a normal-sized Boston Terrier, standing between twelve and seventeen inches. He often weighs between twenty and forty pounds. His exact size will be determined by the dominant parent breed.

The Boglen Terrier is an adaptable little dog. He is happy with younger and older singles, or a family with children of any age. He can acclimate to living in any size apartment, or he can live in a home, with or without a fenced-in yard.

He is highly intelligent, and the hunter instinct of both breeds will be evident in the Boglen Terrier. He is alert and full of energy. He is protective, and he is especially watchful of children, whom he loves. He is gentle yet courageous.

The Boglen Terrier, or Boggle, is known for his loyalty and will defend his master at any given time. He is fearless and will not back down, especially when it comes to his person.

He can be a bit stubborn from time to time, but his other positive characteristics make up for this negative behavior and then some.

It is important to make sure that the Boglen Terrier gets just the right amount of food, which is similar to the food guidelines set forth for a purebred Boston Terrier. The Boglen Terrier has a predisposition to gain weight, so feeding him a nutritionally balanced diet in the correct portions is paramount.

While many of the Boston mixes are fairly easy to train – even though the Boston does tend to be somewhat obstinate at times – the Boglen Terrier does not follow along his fellow designer mixes. The Beagle parent breed lends a bit of his strong will to his hybrid breed progeny. However, if you will remain vigilant and patient, the Boglen Terrier will be successfully trained. Like the Boston Terrier parent breed, the Boglen Terrier is motivated by positive rewards – namely food or treats – so utilize this to your benefit.

Other Boston Terrier Mixes

Technically, the Boston Terrier, like any other breed, can be crossbred with dogs of just about any breed. However, a few mixes are more popular than others. A product of crossbreeding the Siberian Husky and the Boston Terrier produces a hybrid known as the Bosky.

Another popular mix is the American Pit Bull Terrier and the Boston Terrier, known as the Boston Bull Terrier.

The personalities of each of these hybrid dogs are highly unpredictable, and the appearance of the dog is also greatly dependent upon the dominant parent breed. However, most Bosky owners report that their hybrid dogs do not have the trademark blue eyes of the Husky.

A third popular Boston hybrid is the Miniature Schnauzer and the Boston Terrier. This designer breed is known as the Mini Boz/Bos. The Mini Boz often has many traits of the Boston with the characteristic beard of the Schnauzer.

Owners wishing to bring about a smaller Boston Terrier often breed them with small, toy-sized dogs. Known as the Boston Yorkie, the dog generally inherits the long, silky hair of the Yorkie parent with the brachycephalic snout of the Boston Terrier. This hybrid will be small, and you may need to use caution when placing a small dog such as this with younger children.

When the Poodle and the Boston Terrier are interbred, the result is often known as a Boston Doodle. Keep in mind that the breeder often mixes a Boston Terrier with a Miniature Poodle. The Boston Doodle may have the short coat of the Boston and Boston markings with longer hair on his ears, or he may inherit a longer coat and a longer nose compared to the Boston Terrier parent breed.

The Pomston is another popular mixed breed featuring a Boston Terrier and a Pomeranian. The Pomston will often have the short, brachycephalic nose of the Boston Terrier parent breed with longer hair. It is often brindle in color; however, this will depend on the dominant parent breed.

Conclusion

I have been around many types of dogs throughout my life, but I fell in love with the Boston Terrier breed twenty years ago, and I really don't think I could love another breed quite the same. The Boston Terrier is such a joy to live with. He is one of the most loving, loyal breeds. He may also be stubborn, but at the same time, he is highly intelligent and courageous. His stubbornness is really just a part of his being a terrier – often terriers need to be shown just why they need to do what their owner tells them. Also, it is difficult for the Terrier part of the Boston Terrier to forget how wonderful it is to chase squirrels or rabbits; however, the Boston Terrier was not meant to be a hunting dog. He is happiest right with his loving family. He adapts to living almost anywhere, and he is a low-maintenance dog. If he is fed a nutritionally-balanced, high-quality diet, he will remain fairly healthy for a number of years. He is one of the easiest dog breeds to train in spite of his propensity for stubbornness. He will become a member of the family; a position he craves from the day you bring him home.

I have tried to be exhaustive when sharing both my personal knowledge and knowledge that I gained as I researched for this book. Remember, when training your Boston Terrier, begin working with him from day one, and he will be successfully housebroken within a year, sometimes sooner. Be patient with him; it literally breaks the spirit of the Boston Terrier to think that his master is upset with him. The Boston may be very silly at times (and downright goofy), but he is also highly intelligent. He is sensitive to your emotions as well. Perhaps this is why he makes such a great cuddle-buddy; the Boston Terrier just seems to know when you need a little affection as well.

I wish you the best of luck on your journey with your own Boston Terrier. There is a wealth of reputable breeders to choose from. If you choose to adopt an older Boston, you can't go wrong there, either. Bostons simply want to give back their love, and they do not care if you came along later in their lives. Trust your instincts when selecting a reputable breeder; while there are some breeders who simply want to make money from their Boston pups, there are plenty more that love the breed and just want to see their puppies go to good homes.

Enjoy that little bundle of energy!

BONUS!

Your Trusted Resource List

A small compilation of Boston Terrier breeders across the United States:

- http://bestbostonterrierpuppies.com/

  This kennel, located in east Tennessee, adheres to AKC standards and truly strives to improve the breed.

- http://circlejkennels.homestead.com/

  Located in Alabama, the puppies at Circle J Kennels are raised like members of the family! Training is also available at this location.

- http://www.bostonterriernewyork.com/

  This kennel in Long Island, NY offers AKC-registered pups, and, most importantly, medical records from up to five previous generations.

- http://www.tbstutz.com/toba_bostons.html

  Located in New York state, this breeder has extensive experience in breeding according to AKC standards, in addition to years of dog show experience.

- https://bossybostons.com/

  This Midwestern (USA) breeder raises pups in their home, with plenty of early socialization.

- http://www.windhillpuppies.net/

  These breeders are licensed in their home state of Illinois, and their puppies are given optimum vet care prior to leaving for their forever home.

- https://www.thewholedog.org/index-1.html

  This breeder in Northern California offers a variety of health guarantees.

- http://www.daybostonterriers.com/

  This Northern California breeder has nearly three decades of experience, in addition to offering a number of health guarantees.

- http://puppyfinder.com/boston-terrier-puppies-for-sale

  This website verifies the identification of sellers before allowing posts regarding puppies for sale.

Boston Terrier breeders in Canada:

- https://www.canadogs.ca/boston-terrier/

  This is a general website providing a list of breeders of Boston Terriers located in central Canada.

- http://puppysites.com/breed/bostonterrier/breeder_canadaontario/

  This website offers a list of trusted breeders in Ontario, Canada.

- https://www.chapmanbostonterriers.com/

  This breeder, located in Ontario Bay, raises Boston pups in the home as a member of the family. These pups are raised with children and other dogs – perfect early socialization!

Boston Terrier Breeders in the United Kingdom:

- https://www.champdogs.co.uk/breeds/boston-terrier/breeders

  This website offers a comprehensive list of Boston Terrier breeders in the United Kingdom.

- http://www.wilharman.co.uk/

  This breeder, located in Lincolnshire, is a member of several conformation clubs, and the goal of their breeding program is to continually improve the breed.

- http://www.ringablok.co.uk/

  This kennel, located in South Wales, offers offspring of dogs trained for the show ring.

- https://www.thekennelclub.org.uk/services/public/findapuppy/Default.aspx?id=Boston+Terrier

  This website offers a comprehensive list of Boston Terrier breeders throughout the U.K. Breeders must meet certain standards before they are allowed to advertise on the site.

Boston Terrier Rescues in the United States:

- http://btrescue.org/tn/

  This Boston Terrier rescue is located in eastern TN, and it works with sister rescue operations in Alabama and Kentucky.

- http://midwestbtrescue.org/adopt-me/illinois-dogs

  This Boston Terrier rescue serves the states of Michigan, Illinois, Ohio, and Indiana.

- https://www.bostonrescue.net/

  This website lists reputable Boston Terrier rescues throughout the United States.

- http://bostonterrier.rescueme.org/California
  This Boston Terrier rescue serves the entire state of California.

Boston Terrier Rescues in Canada:

- https://www.bostonterrierrescuecanada.com/
  This Boston Terrier Rescue works to place Boston Terriers, and Boston Terrier mixes throughout Canada.

Boston Terrier Rescues in the United Kingdom:

- http://www.ukbostonterrierrescue.co.uk/
  This breed-specific non-profit rescue organization specializes in rehoming Boston Terriers.

Boston Terrier Clubs/Dog Fanciers in the United States:

- http://bostonterrierclubofamerica.org/
  This club is dedicated to the improvement of the Boston Terrier breed. One can find breed standards, links to local clubs, and guidelines for showing a Boston Terrier.
- http://www.akc.org/dog-breeds/boston-terrier/
  The American Kennel Club website lists conformation standards for the Boston Terrier.
- https://www.continentalkennelclub.com/
  This organization also provides an alternative registration for Boston Terriers.

Boston Terrier Clubs/Dog Fanciers in Canada:

- http://www.bostonterrierclubofcanada.com/
  This is the sister club of the Boston Terrier Club of America.

- https://www.ckc.ca/en/Choosing-a-Dog/Choosing-a-Breed/Non-Sporting-Dogs/Boston-Terrier

  The Canadian Kennel Club website provides a wealth of information regarding breed standards and local clubs.

Boston Terrier Clubs/Dog Fanciers in the United Kingdom:

- http://thebostonterrierclub.co.uk/

  This club sponsors two open dog shows and one championship show per year.

Made in United States
North Haven, CT
06 November 2021

10909356R00075